CONTIENE (CONTENTS)

ISBN 0-634-01826-4

HAL•LEONARD
CORPORATION

7777 W. BLUEMOUND RD. P.O. BOX 13819 MILWAUKEE, WI 53213

Visit Hal Leonard Online at
www.halleonard.com

Acércate Más
(Come Closer to Me)

Registration 3
Rhythm: Rhumba or Latin

Music and Spanish Words by Osvaldo Farres
English Words by Al Stewart

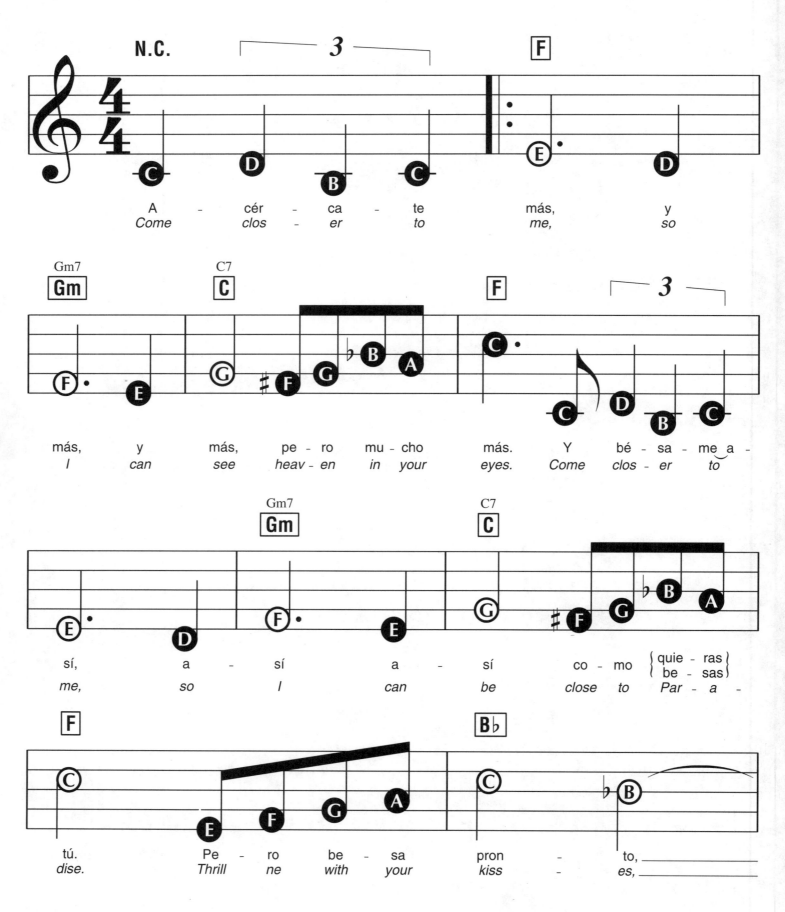

222222

22222222222222

Copyright © 1940, 1945 by Peer International Corporation
Copyrights Renewed
International Copyright Secured   All Rights Reserved

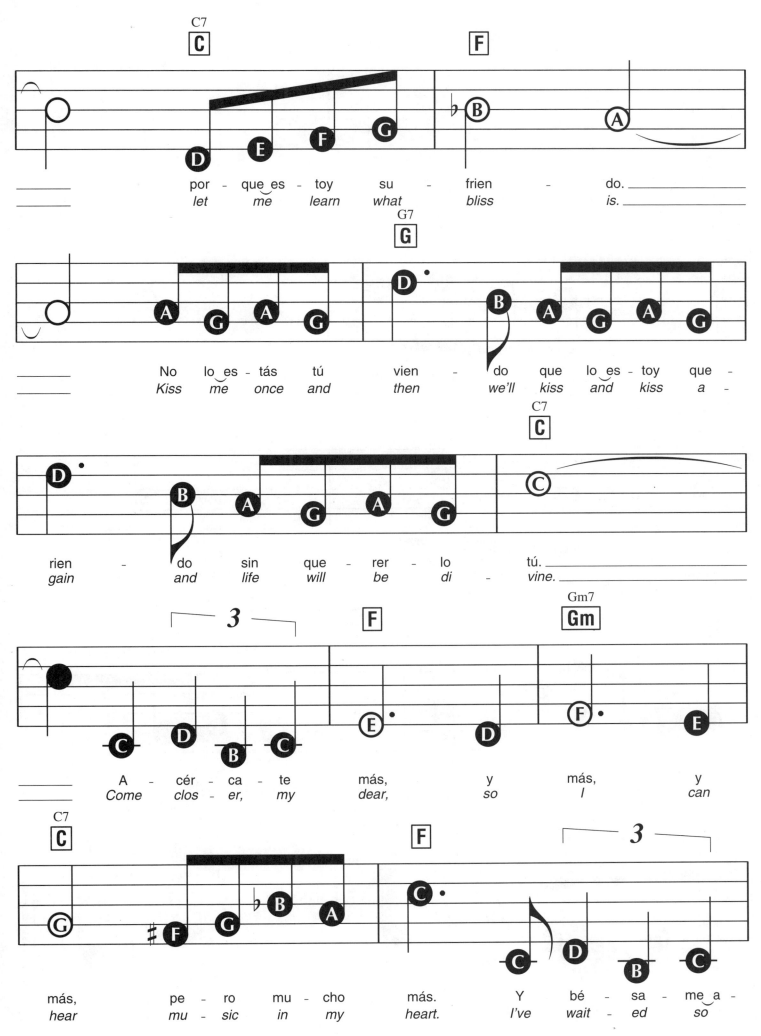

3

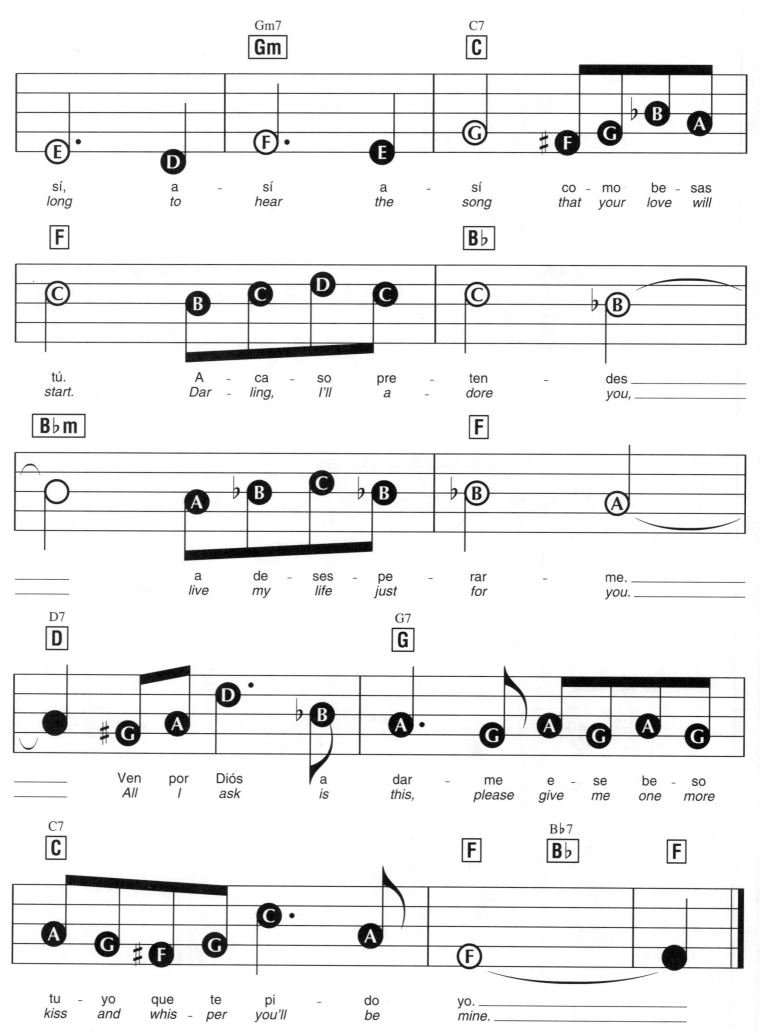

Amor
(Amor, Amor, Amor)

Registration 4
Rhythm: Rhumba or Latin

Music by Gabriel Ruiz
Spanish Words by Ricardo Lopez Mendez
English Words by Norman Newell

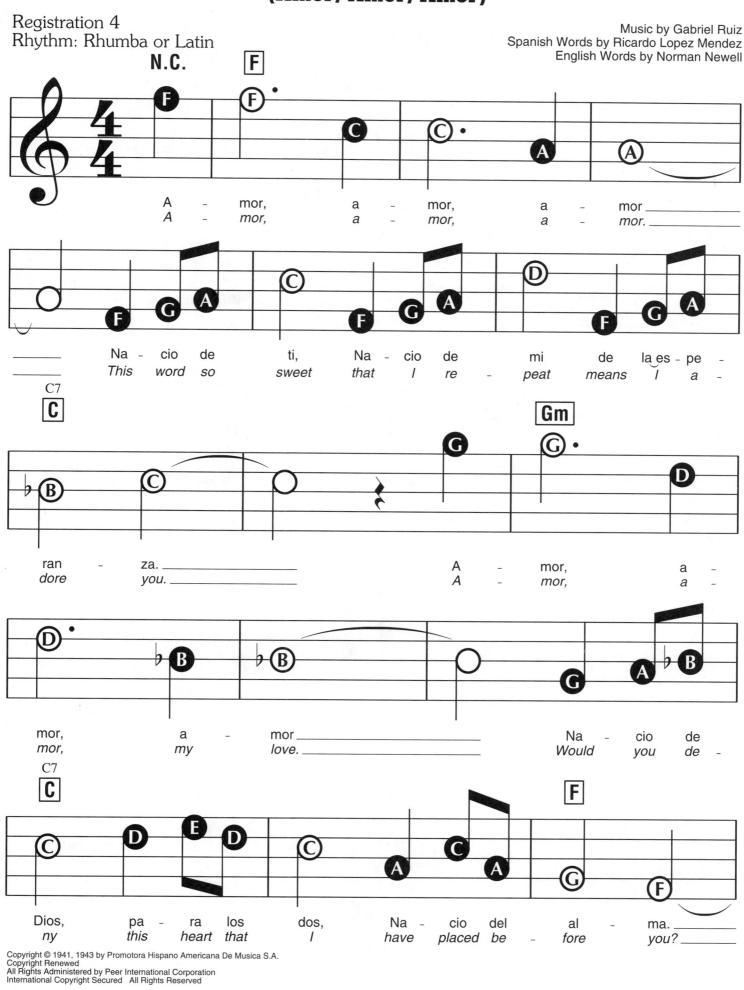

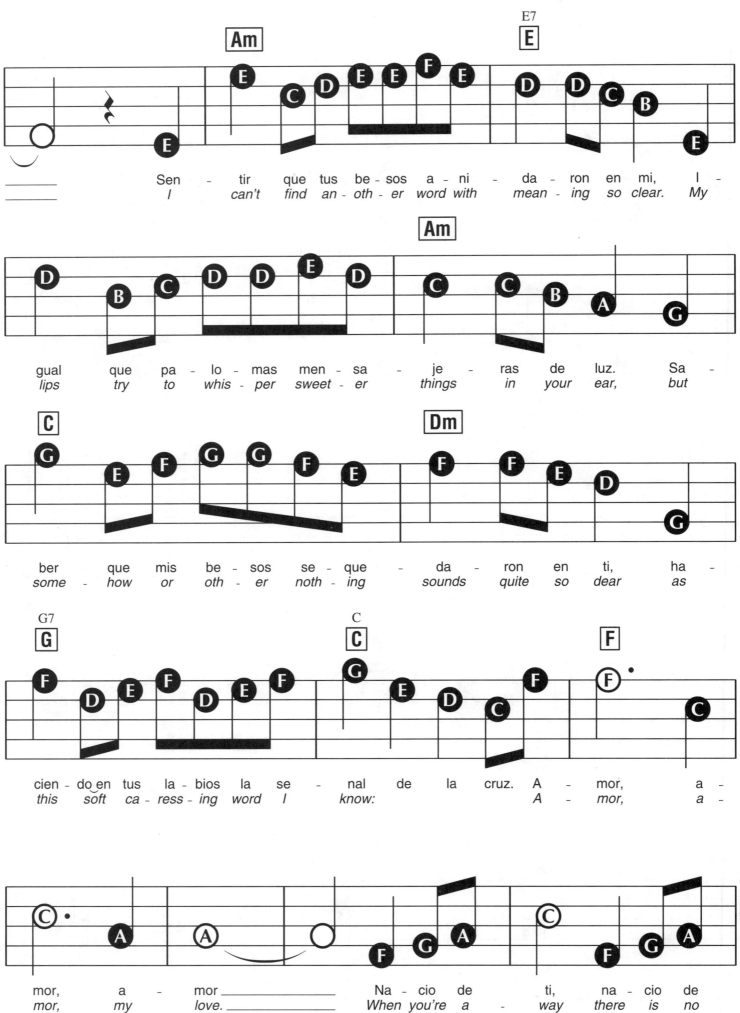

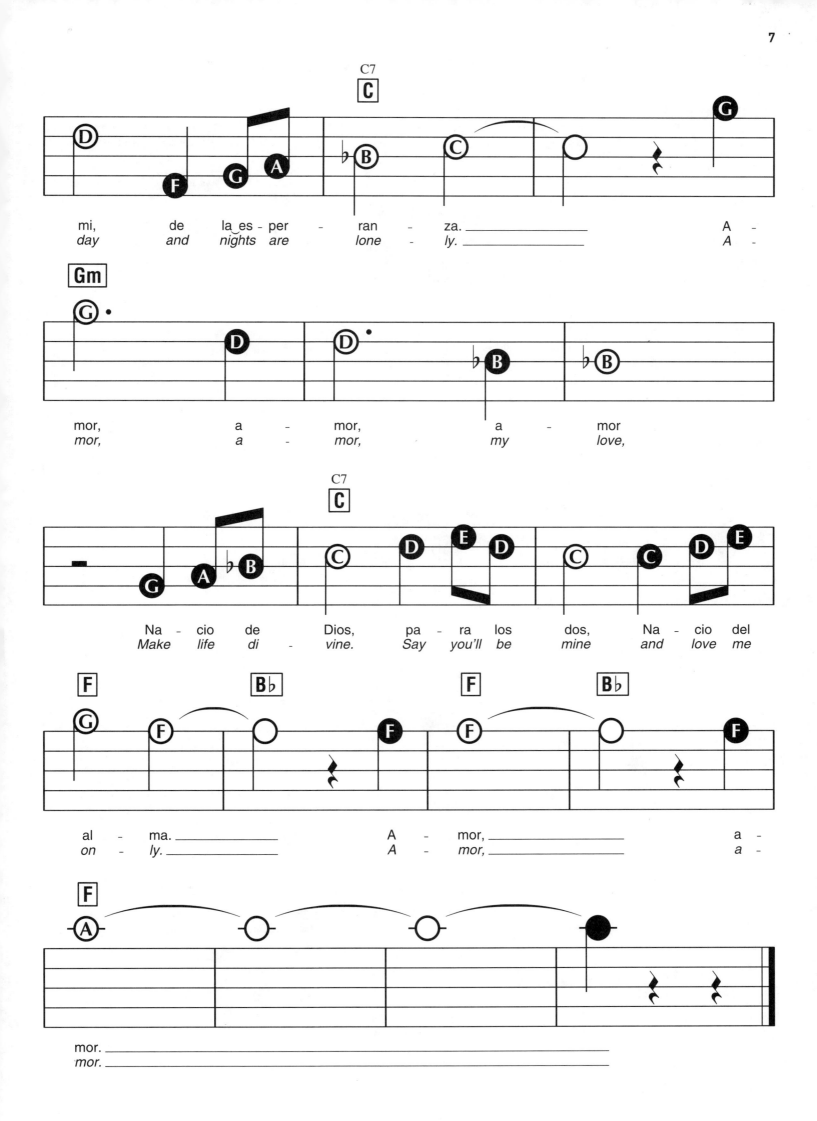

Aquellos Ojos Verdes
(Green Eyes)

Registration 3
Rhythm: Rhumba or Latin

Music by Nilo Menendez
Spanish Words by Adolfo Utrera
English Words by E. Rivera and E. Woods

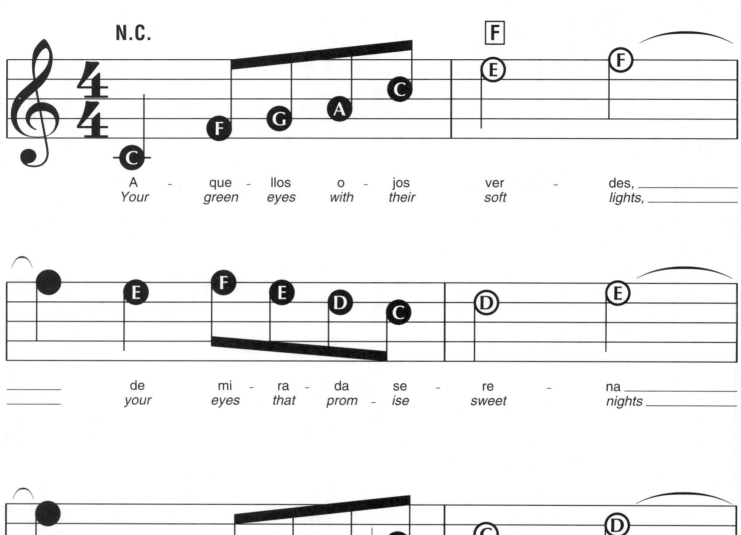

A - que - llos o - jos ver - des, _____
Your green eyes with their soft lights, _____

_____ de mi - ra - da se - re - na _____
your eyes that prom - ise sweet nights _____

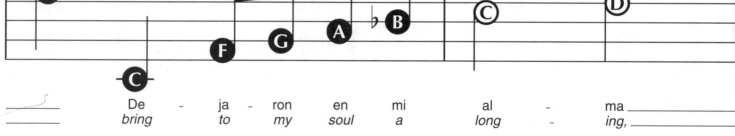

_____ De - ja - ron en mi al - ma
bring to my soul a long - ing,

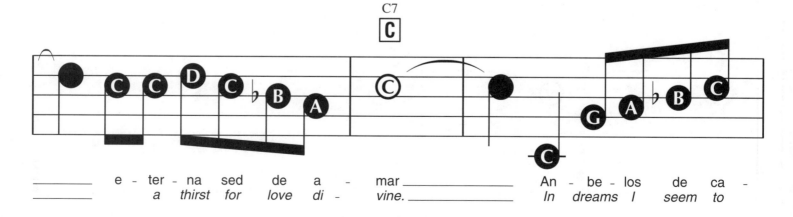

_____ e - ter - na sed de a - mar _____ An - be - los de ca -
a thirst for love di - vine. _____ In dreams I seem to

9

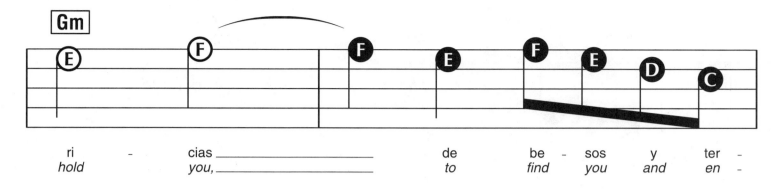

ri - cias _____ de be - sos y ter -
hold you, _____ to find you and en -

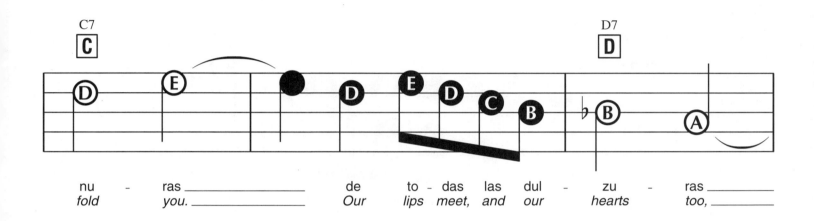

nu - ras _____ de to - das las dul - zu - ras _____
fold you. _____ Our lips meet, and our hearts too, _____

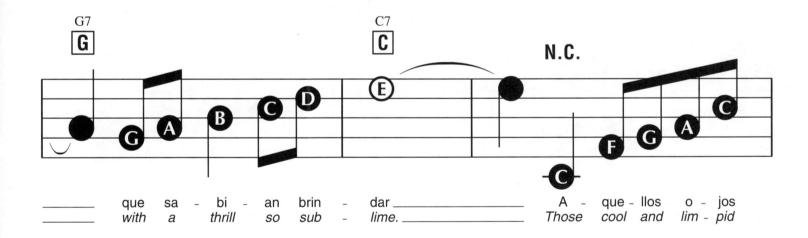

_____ que sa - bi - an brin - dar _____ A - que - llos o - jos
_____ with a thrill so sub - lime. _____ Those cool and lim - pid

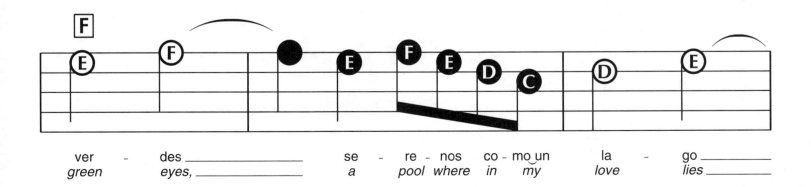

ver - des _____ se - re - nos co - mo un la - go _____
green eyes, _____ a pool where in my love lies _____

10

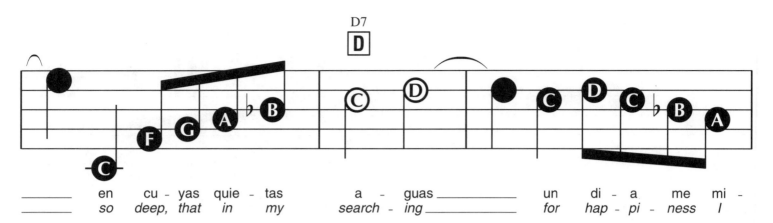

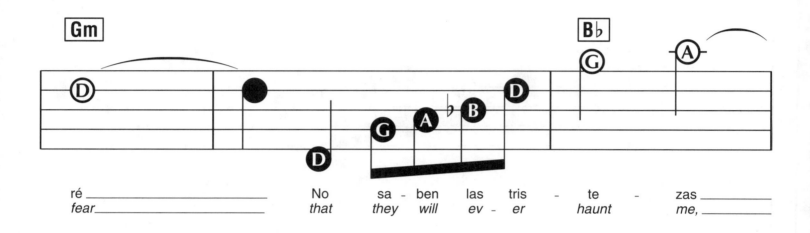

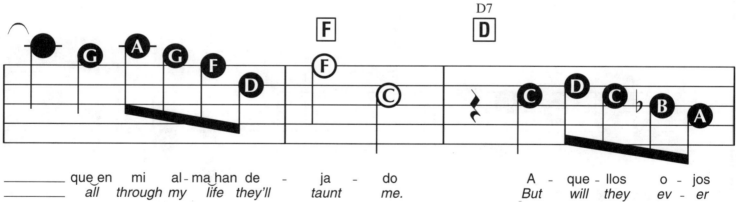

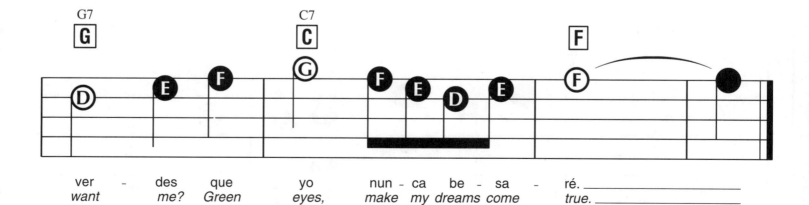

El Reloj

Registration 3
Rhythm: Rhumba or Latin

Words and Music by
Roberto Cantoral

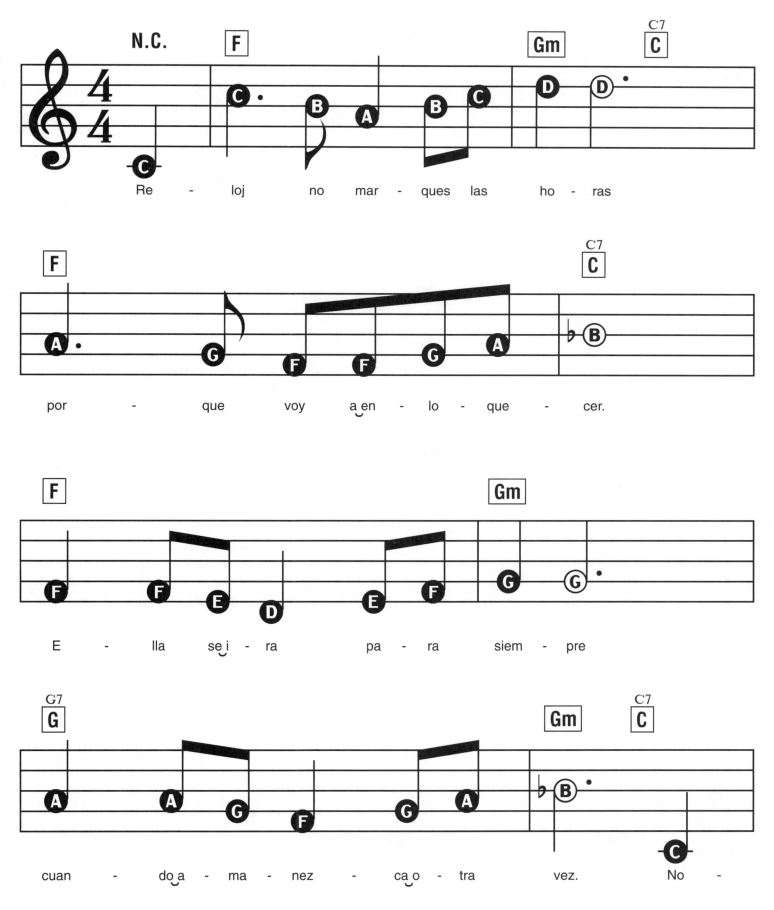

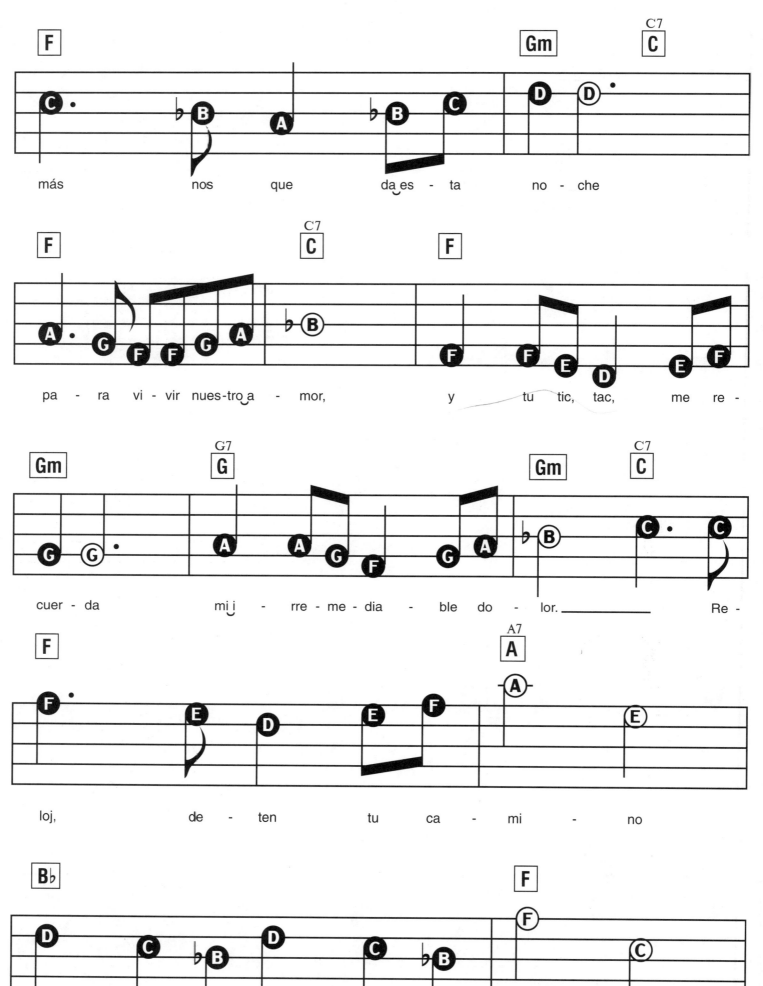

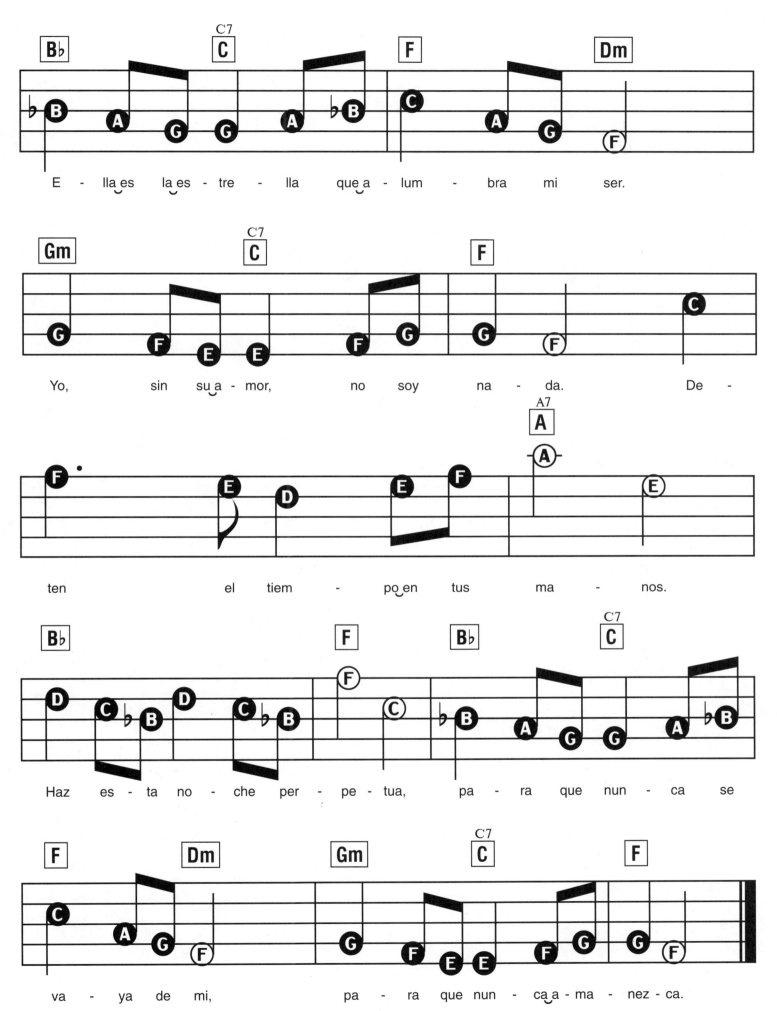

Bésame Mucho
(Kiss Me Much)

Registration 1
Rhythm: Rhumba or Latin

Music and Spanish Words by Consuelo Velazquez
English Words by Sunny Skylar

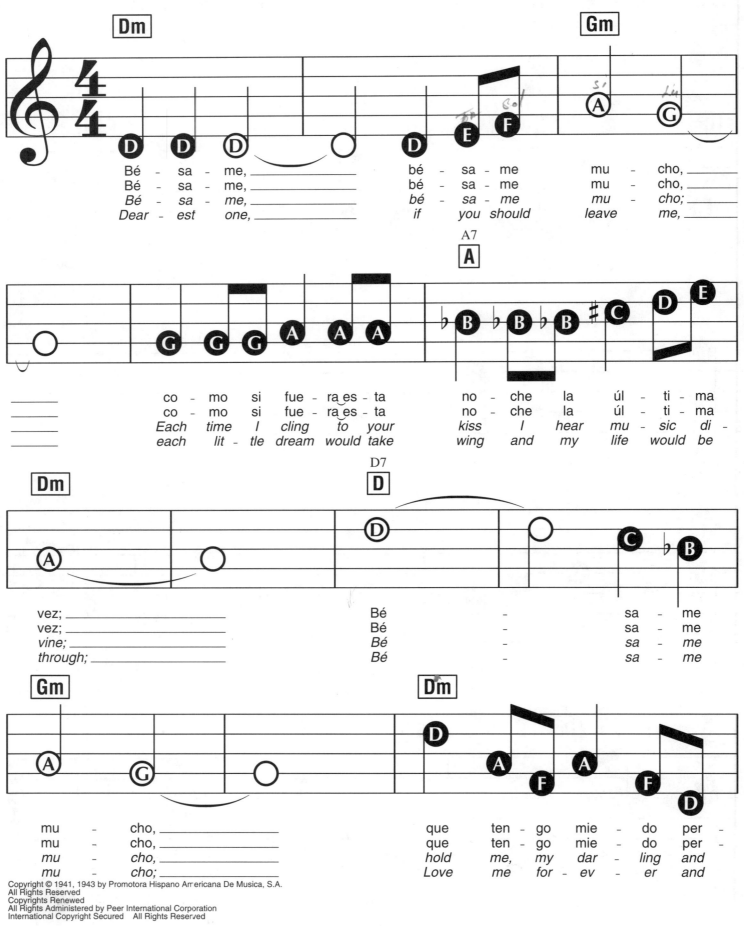

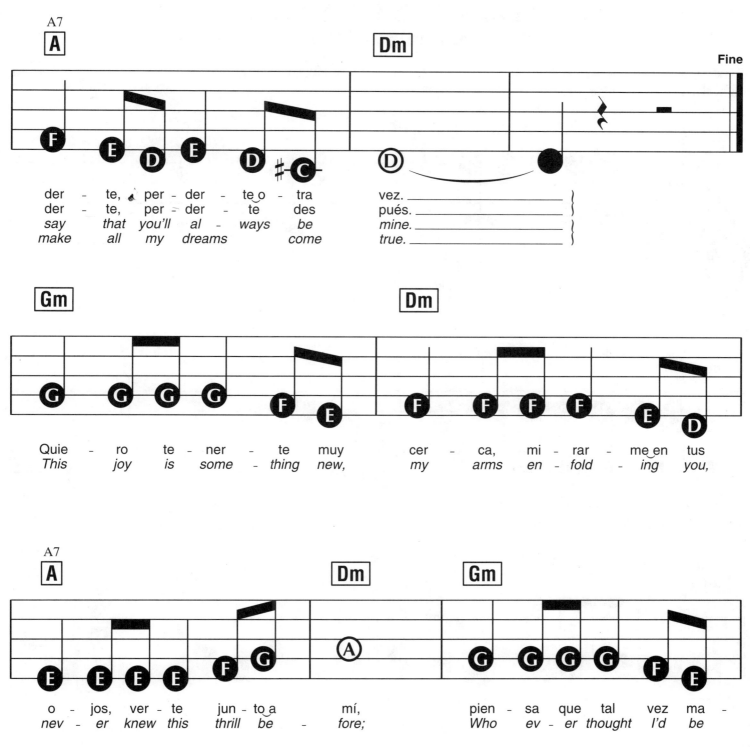

A7
A　　　　　　　　　　　　　　　**Dm**　　　　　　　　　　**Fine**

der – te, per – der – te o – tra　vez. _____
der – te, per – der – te des　pués. _____
say　that you'll al – ways　be　mine. _____
make　all　my　dreams　come　true. _____

Gm　　　　　　　　　　　　　　　**Dm**

Quie – ro te – ner – te muy　cer – ca, mi – rar – me en tus
This　joy　is　some – thing new,　my　arms en – fold – ing　you,

A7
A　　　　　　　　　　　**Dm**　　　**Gm**

o – jos, ver – te jun – to a　mí,　pien – sa que tal vez ma –
nev – er knew this thrill be – fore;　Who ev – er thought I'd be

D.C. al Fine
(Return to beginning
Play to Fine)

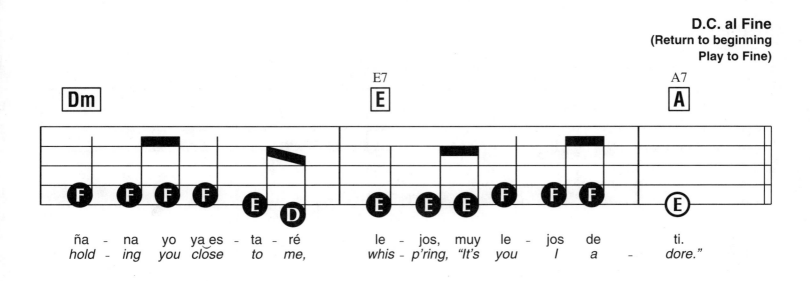

Dm　　　　　　　　　E7　　　　　　　　　A7
　　　　　　　　　　　　E　　　　　　　　**A**

ña – na yo ya es – ta – ré　le – jos, muy le – jos de　ti.
hold – ing you close to me,　whis – p'ring, "It's you I a – dore."

Cuando Caliente El Sol
(Love Me with All Your Heart)

Registration 9
Rhythm: Rhumba or Latin

Original Words and Music by Carlos Rigual and Carlos A. Martinoli
English Words by Sunny Skylar

Cuan - do ca - lien - ta el sol _____ a - qui en la pla - ya
Love me with all your heart, _____ that's all I want, love.

sien - to tu cuer - po vi - brar cer - ca de mí, _____
Love me with all of your heart or not at all. _____

es tu pal - pi - tar _____ es tu ca - ra es tu pe - lo son tus
Just prom - ise me this: _____ that you'll give me all your kiss - es, Ev - 'ry

be - sos me es - tre - mez - co - o - o - o.
win - ter, ev - 'ry sum - mer, ev - 'ry fall.

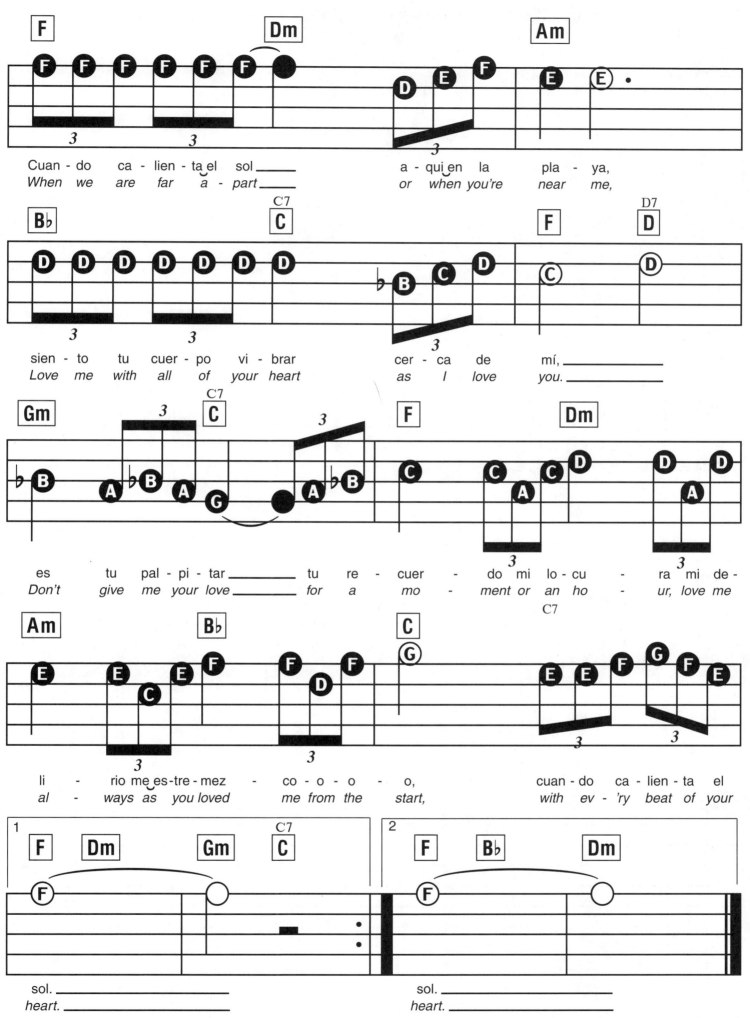

Cuando Se Quiere De Veras
(Yours)

Registration 2
Rhythm: Rhumba or Latin

Words by Albert Gamse and Jack Sherr
Music by Gonzalo Roig

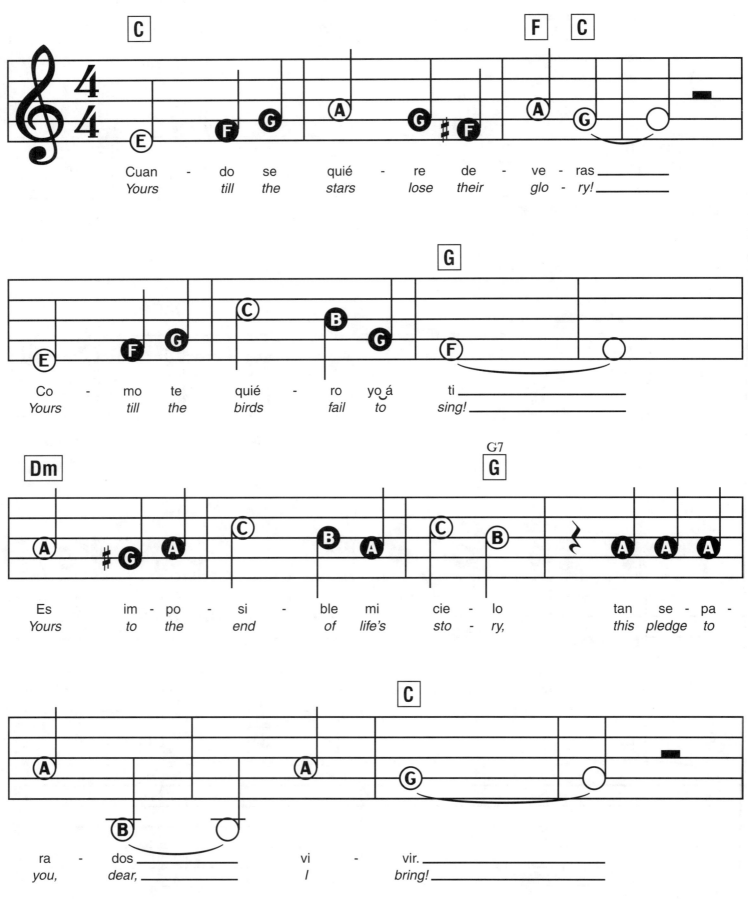

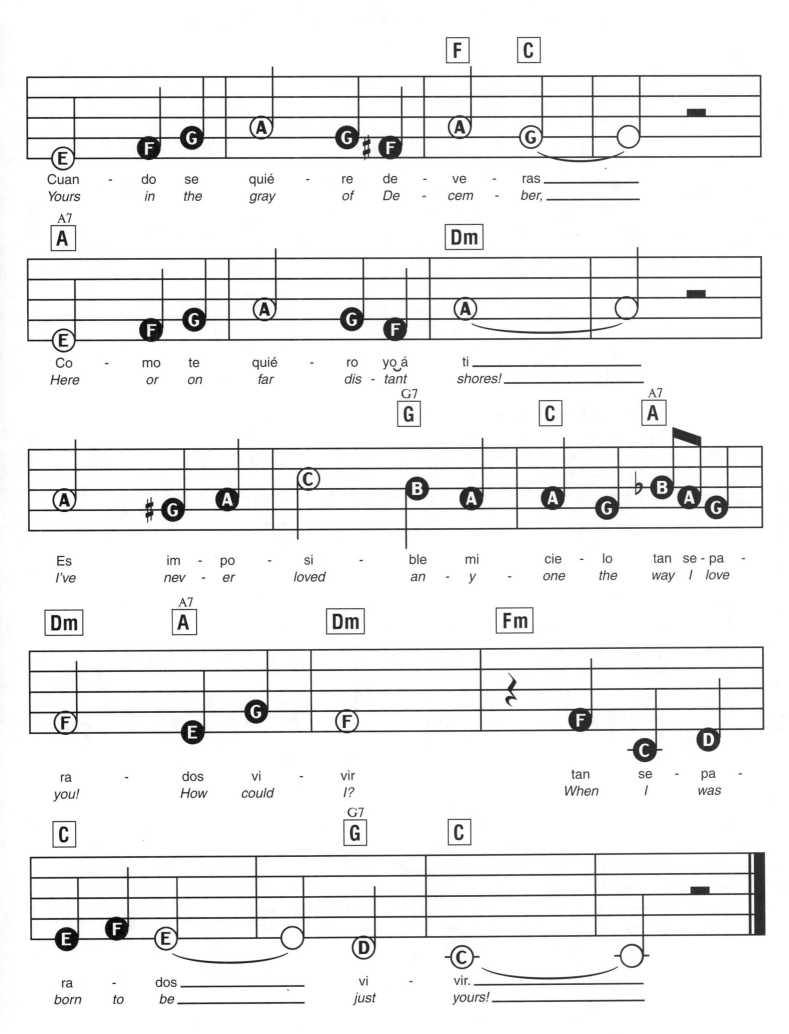

Inolvidable

Registration 1
Rhythm: Rhumba or Latin

Words and Music by
Julio Gutierrez

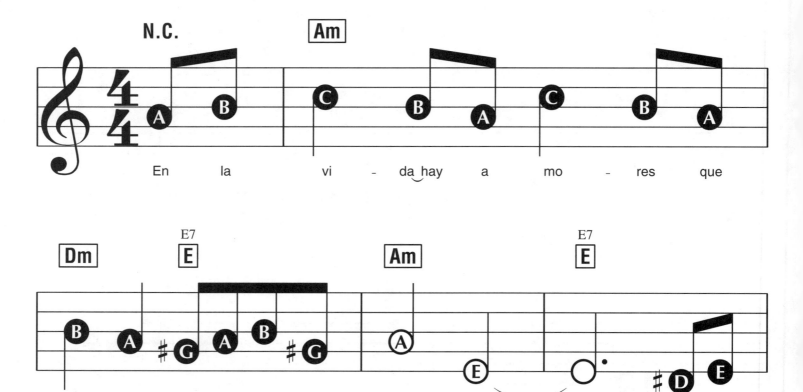

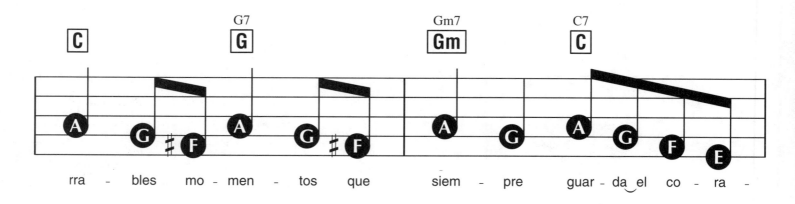

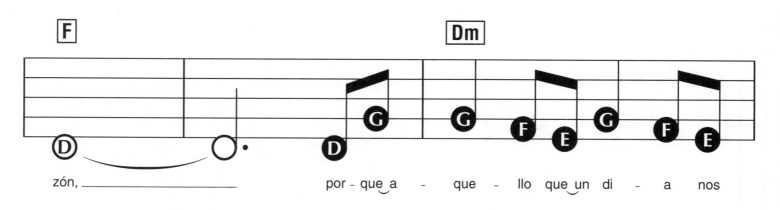

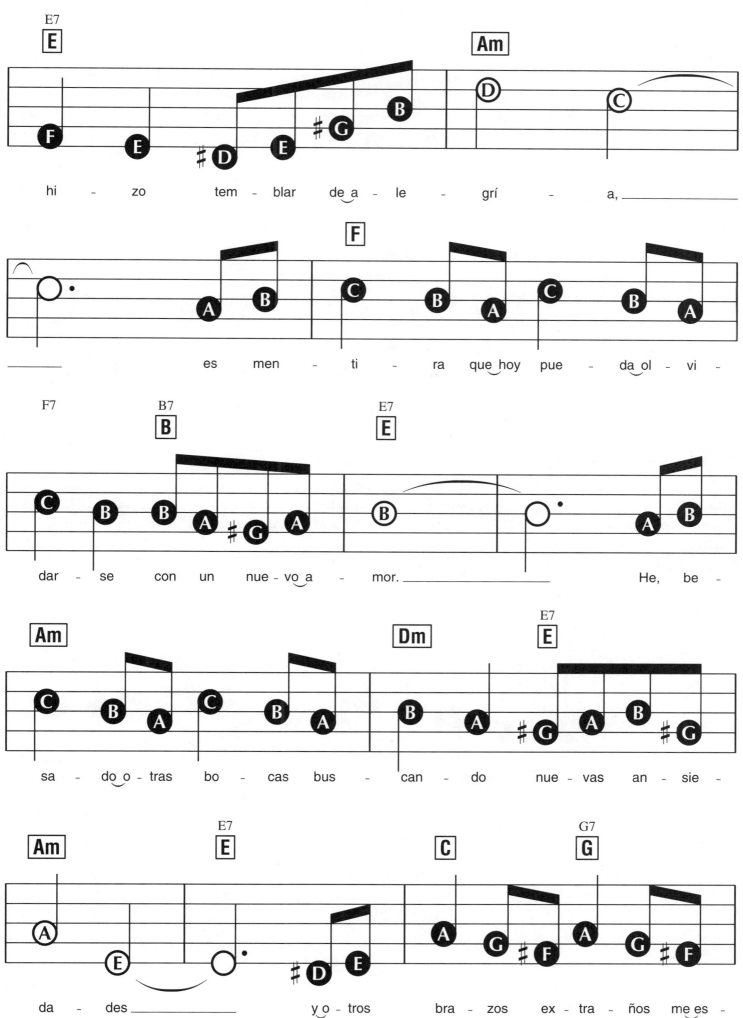

22

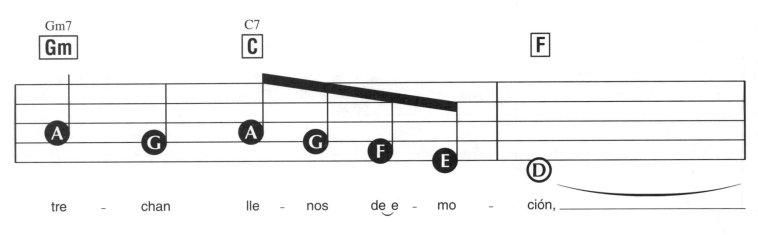

tre – chan lle – nos de e mo – ción, _____

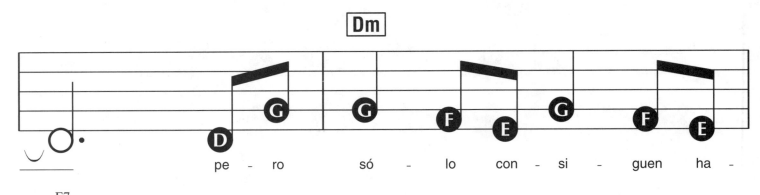

pe – ro só – lo con – si – guen ha –

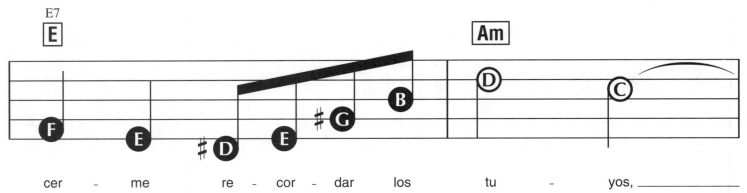

cer – me re – cor – dar los tu – yos, _____

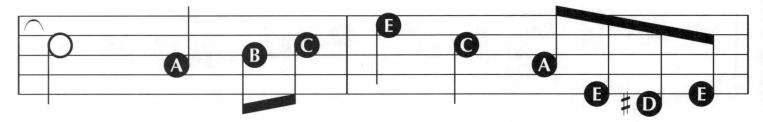

que i – nol – vi – da – ble – men – te vi – vi –

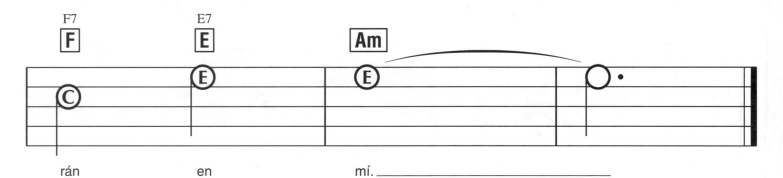

rán en mí. _____

Noche De Ronda
(Be Mine Tonight)

Registration 3
Rhythm: Waltz

Original Words and Music by Maria Teresa Lara
English Words by Sunny Skylar

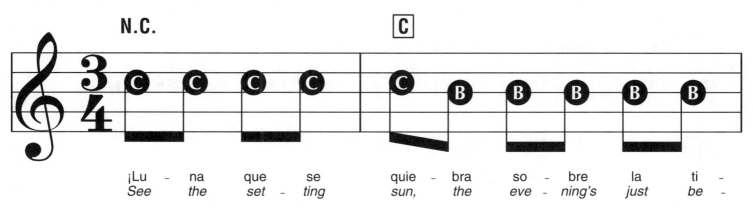

¡Lu - na que se quie - bra so - bre la ti -
See the set - ting sun, the eve - ning's just be -

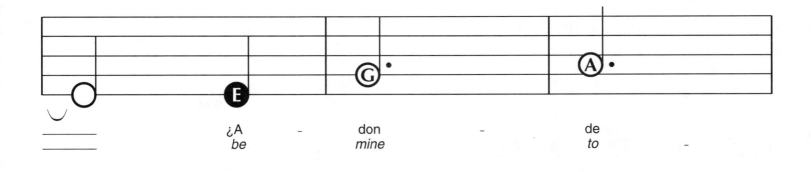

nie - bla de mi so - le - dad! _____
gun and love is in the air: _____

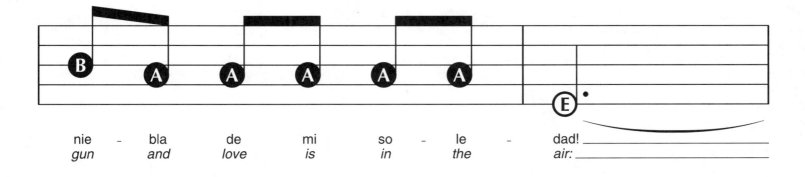

¿A - don - de
be mine to -

G7

G

vas? _____ ¿Di - me si es - ta
night. _____ At a time like

24

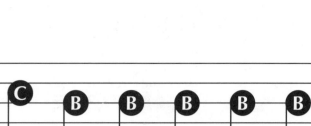
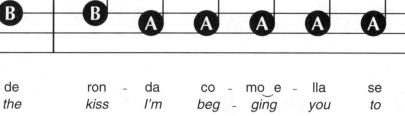

no - che tú te vas de ron - da co - mo e - lla se
this, would you re - fuse the kiss I'm beg - ging you to

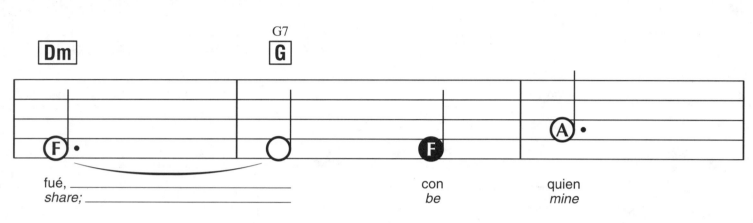

fué, _____ con quien
share; _____ be mine

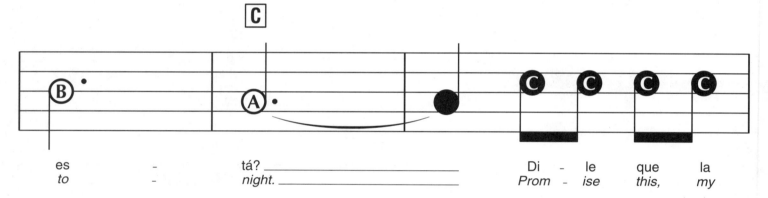

es - tá? _____ Di le que la
to - night. _____ Prom - ise this, my

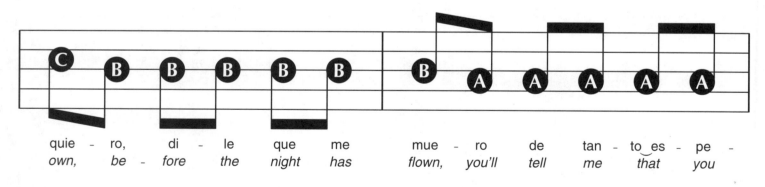

quie - ro, di - le que me mue - ro de tan - to es - pe -
own, be - fore the night has flown, you'll de tell me that you

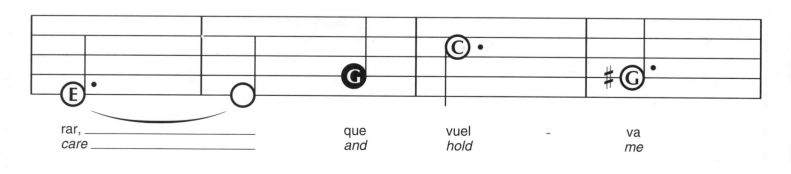

rar, _____ que vuel - va
care _____ and hold me

FOR ORGANS, PIANOS & ELECTRONIC KEYBOARDS

E-Z PLAY® TODAY

The World's Biggest and Best-Selling Songbook Series!

E-Z Play Today chord notation is designed for playing standard chord positions or single key chords on all major brand organs and portable keyboards.

With over 300 outstanding books in this series, **E-Z PLAY TODAY** is the shortest distance between beginning music and playing fun! Here are some reasons why you should play E-Z PLAY TODAY:

- World's largest series of music folios
- Full-size books – large 9" x 12" format features easy-to-read, easy-to-play music
- Accurate arrangements: simple enough for the beginner, but with accurate chords and melody lines.
- Minimum number of page turns
- Thousands of songs – an incredible array of favorites, plus special BEGINNINGS instruction books
- Easy-to-play arrangements progress to double-note arrangements in many books
- Eye-catching, full-color covers
- Lyrics – most arrangements include words and music
- Most up-to-date registrations – books in the series contain a general registration guide, as well as individual song rhythm suggestions
- Guitar Chord Chart – all songs in the series can also be played on guitar, and many E-Z PLAY TODAY songbooks include a guitar chord chart
- Alphabetical Songfinder lists thousands of songs in the series and the books in which they can be found
- Catalog – many books include an insert listing all other books available in the series

BEGINNINGS SERIES

Beginnings Book A is now available with audio accompaniments! The CD and cassette feature instruction and examples of all the songs in the book to play along with!

Beginnings – Book A
An introduction to the E-Z Play Today Music Series with 13 great songs, including: When the Saints Go Marching In • Kumbaya • Beautiful Brown Eyes • Londonderry Air • I Gave My Love a Cherry • and more. Also includes Keyboard Guides and Pedal Labels.
00100320 Book Only $5.95
00100015 Book/CD Pack $12.95
00100014 Book/Cassette Pack $9.95
00100423 Fundamentos Musicales (Spanish Text) $5.95

Beginnings – Book B
Continues the instruction from Book A to provide the player with more advanced techniques. Features 18 more great tunes.
00100319..$5.95

Beginnings – Book C
Explains how to improvise E-Z Play Today arrangements. 12 songs: All Through the Night • Amazing Grace • Andantino • Dark Eyes • Fascination • Give My Regards to Broadway • and more!
00100318..$5.95

Beginnings Supplementary Songbook
This supplementary songbook works with instruction books A, B, and C in BEGINNINGS FOR KEYBOARDS. Includes 28 super songs, including: Crazy • Edelweiss • Memory • Stand by Me • and more.
00101496..$5.95

Beginnings Composite
A comprehensive instruction course that includes Beginnings A, B, and C, and Supplementary Songbook.
00100317..$19.95

EXPLORING SERIES
Explore new techniques to enhance your playing with this unique series. These books explain how to use keyboard functions to improve your sound and different playing techniques to spice up songs. Each book includes great songs so you learn as you play.

E1. Exploring Automatic Rhythms
A special edition teaching new techniques and various features of automatic rhythms on the electronic keyboard. Includes 12 songs: America • Can't Help Falling in Love • Neutron Dance • What Child Is This? • more.
00102102..$5.95

E2. Exploring Chords
This edition teaches "fingered" chords. Includes 252 chord diagrams; explains what fingered chords are and how they are played; and presents charts of the most common fingered chords for every note of the scale and in every position. Includes eight great songs: Bewitched • Everytime You Go Away • I Left My Heart in San Francisco • If You Remember Me • In the Mood • Love Is Here to Stay • Some Enchanted Evening • This Nearly Was Mine.
00102103..$6.95

E3. Exploring Playing Techniques
This book lets electronic keyboard players in on "tricks" to enhance their playing techniques. It teaches the player how to add variety and interest to any song by changing registration, adding grace notes, etc. Thirteen songs, including: Amazing Grace • And I Love Her • The Rainbow Connection • more.
00102104..$5.95

E4. Exploring Intros and Endings
This book reveals some of the secrets of the pros in creating introductions and endings for arrangements played on electronic keyboards. Includes 11 songs: Another Somebody Done Somebody Wrong Song • Can't Help Falling in Love • Climb Ev'ry Mountain • Endless Love • and more.
00102105..$5.95

E5. Exploring Double Notes
This supplementary book gives the keyboard player instruction on double notes, including the correct notes to play and how to come up with your own double note harmonies. It features 14 great tunes: Don't Cry for Me Argentina • Kumbaya • Somewhere Out There • The Entertainer • more.
00102106..$5.95

E6. Exploring Right Hand Chords
This book cuts through most of the technical material and gets right to the heart of how to add full chords to the melodies you play. Includes 14 songs: A Bicycle Built for Two • Could I Have This Dance • Down in the Valley • Fascination • The Longest Time • Sweet Caroline • The Wonder of You • more.
00102107..$5.95

E7. Exploring Backing Tracks
Experience the fun of overdubbing with your keyboard's sequencer! This book teaches how to read backing tracks in an arrangement, how to record backing tracks into a sequencer, and how to use backing tracks as duets to play live. Nine songs, including: Getting to Know You • I Write the Songs • Somewhere Out There • Stand by Me • and more.
00102112..$5.95

E-Z Play Today Organ Keyboard Guides
Sturdy cardboard guides to help you quickly and easily learn the keyboard!
00100519..$2.50

KID'S KEYBOARD COURSE

The Fun Way to Learn!

Book 1
This book teaches children how to use an electronic keyboard through easy instruction, color-coded notation and stickers, lots of illustrations, games and puzzles, and plenty of songs that kids will be able to play right away.
00102133...$5.95

Book 2
This book picks up the instruction where Book 1 lets off and gets students into more aspects of making music. Like Book 1, it also contains lots of songs, puzzles, illustrations and fun!
00102134...$5.95

GETTING STARTED

A Beginner's Learning Guide for All Electronic Keyboards

A clear and easy guide to getting the most out of your new electronic keyboard. The book contains easy instruction on playing techniques and using electronic keyboard features to enhance your playing. Includes songs that use the techniques demonstrated in the lessons, and comes complete with ABC key stickers to help you remember note names.
00001079...$5.95

E-Z PLAY TODAY SONGBOOKS

1. Favorite Songs with Three Chords
Features 40 easy-to-play favorites, including: Amazing Grace • America • Blue Danube Waltz • Kumbaya • Ode to Joy • Yellow Rose of Texas • and many more.
00102278...$7.95

2. Country Sound
27 country classics, including: Green, Green Grass of Home • Hey, Good Lookin' • I Fall to Pieces • Jambalaya • King of the Road • Make the World Go Away • Your Cheatin' Heart • and more.
00100374...$8.95

3. Disney's The Hunchback of Notre Dame
10 delightful songs complete with full-color illustrations from the film. Songs include: God Help the Outcasts • Out There • Someday • and more.
00100029...$12.95

4. Dance Band Greats
21 greats, including: Cherry Pink and Apple Blossom White • Fly Me to the Moon • Harbor Lights • In the Mood • Love Me or Leave Me • The Things We Did Last Summer.
00100382...$6.95

5. All-Time Standards
Over 25 standards, including: For Sentimental Reasons • Everybody Loves My Baby • Harlem Nocturne • Memories of You • Que Sera Sera • Tangerine • Undecided • What a Diff'rence a Day Made • When I Fall in Love • and more.
00100305...$6.95

6. Giant Hits
21 Beatles songs, including: All My Loving • And I Love Her • Can't Buy Me Love • Eleanor Rigby • Get Back • A Hard Day's Night • Hey Jude • Let It Be • Michelle • Norwegian Wood • Yellow Submarine • Yesterday.
00100428...$5.95

7. Hits from Musicals
21 hits, including: As Long As He Needs Me • How Are Things in Glocca Morra • I Could Write a Book • I've Grown Accustomed to Her Face • Gonna Build a Mountain • Manhattan • More • On a Clear Day • Summertime • Wouldn't It Be Loverly.
00100442...$5.95

8. Patriotic Songs
21 tunes, including: America • America the Beautiful • Battle Hymn of the Republic • Dixie • God Bless America • Star Spangled Banner • This Is My Country • This Land Is Your Land • Yellow Rose of Texas • You're a Grand Old Flag.
00100490...$5.95

9. Christmas Time
21 favorites, including: Away in a Manger • Deck the Halls • The First Noel • God Rest Ye Merry Gentlemen • Hark! The Herald Angels Sing • It Came Upon a Midnight Clear • Jingle Bells • Joy to the World • O Christmas Tree • O Come All Ye Faithful • Silent Night.
00100355...$5.95

10. Hawaiian Songs
21 Polynesian songs, including: Aloha Oe • The Breeze and I • Hawaiian Wedding Song • The Moon of Manakoora • Now Is the Hour • Pearly Shells • Quiet Village • Sea Breeze • Song of the Islands • Tiny Bubbles.
00100435...$6.95

12. Danceable Favorites
21 songs, including: Downtown • I'll Never Smile Again • It's Not Unusual • Let It Be Me • My Love • Quiet Nights of Quiet Stars • Strangers in the Night • A Sunday Kind of Love • Till Then.
00100386...$6.95

13. Celebrated Favorites – 2nd Edition
20 favorites, including: Ain't Misbehavin' • For Me and My Gal • I Can't Give You Anything But Love • I've Got the World on a String • Kansas City • The Sheik of Araby • Star Dust • That's My Desire • When You're Smiling • and more.
00100345...$6.95

14. All-Time Requests
21 requests, including: April Showers • Blueberry Hill • Heartaches • I Don't Know Why • I'll Get By • I Talk to the Trees • The Old Piano Roll Blues • Too Close for Comfort • What Kind of Fool Am I? • You Can't Be True Dear.
00100300...$5.95

15. Country Pickin's - Third Edition
25 choice country favorites: Any Time • Could I Have This Dance • The Gambler • Hello Walls • I Walk the Line • Jambalaya • Luckenbach, Texas • Rocky Top • more.
00100370...$7.95

16. Broadway's Best
21 show tunes, including: Bali Ha'i • Climb Ev'ry Mountain • Edelweiss • My Favorite Things • Oh What a Beautiful Mornin' • Some Enchanted Evening • The Sound of Music • The Surrey with the Fringe on Top • The Sweetest Sounds • Younger Than Springtime.
00100335...$7.95

17. Fireside Singalong
24 singalongs, including: Alouette • Bicycle Built for Two • Blue Tail Fly • Clementine • For He's a Jolly Good Fellow • Hail, Hail the Gang's All Here • I Love You Truly • I've Been Working on the Railroad • My Bonnie • She'll Be Comin' Round the Mountain.
00100415...$5.95

18. Classical Portraits
21 classical themes, including: Blue Danube Waltz • Brahm's Lullaby • Fantasie Impromptu • Humoresque • Liebestraum • Poet and Peasant Overture • Reverie • Romeo and Juliet • Tales from the Vienna Woods • Vienna Life.
00100362...$5.95

19. Polka and March Beats
21 polkas and marches, including: Barbara Polka • Clarinet Polka • Helena Polka • High School • Cadets • Julida Polka • King Cotton March • Pizzacato Polka • Semper Fidelis • Sharpshooters March • Tinker Polka.
00100540...$5.95

20. Hymns
28 hymns, featuring: Amazing Grace • Kumbaya • Holy, Holy, Holy • Rock of Ages • What a Friend We Have in Jesus • and more.
00102277...$5.95

21. Singalong Standards
21 standards, including: After the Ball • Bill Bailey, Won't You Please Come Home • Give My Regards to Broadway • Ida • In My Merry Oldsmobile • In the Good Old Summertime • Mary's a Grand Old Name • My Wild Irish Rose • Sidewalks of New York • Sweet Adeline • Wait 'Til the Sun Shines, Nellie.
00100578...$5.95

22. Sacred Sounds
32 well-known hymns, including: Blessed Be the Tie That Binds • Crown Him with Many Crowns • Faith of Our Fathers • Give Me That Old-Time Religion • The Old Rugged Cross • Onward, Christian Soldiers • Rock of Ages • Swing Low, Sweet Chariot • Were You There?
00100570...$6.95

23. Disney Spotlights
17 hits, including: The Ballad of Davy Crockett • The Bare Necessities • Chim Chim Cher-ee • Never Smile at a Crocodile • Once Upon a Dream • Peter Pan • Supercalifragilisticexpialidocious • You Can Fly! You Can Fly! You Can Fly!
00100405...$6.95

24. (The Magic of) M-I-C-K-E-Y
17 selections, including: Bibbidi-Bobbidi Boo • A Dream Is a Wish Your Heart Makes • I'm Late • It's a Small World • Mickey Mouse March • No Other Love • The Unbirthday Song • Westward Ho The Wagons!
00100480...$5.95

25. Disney Dazzle
17 favorites, including: Give a Little Whistle • Heigh-Ho, Heigh-Ho • I'm Wishing • Lavender Blue • Some Day My Prince Will Come • When You Wish Upon a Star • Whistle While You Work • Who's Afraid of the Big Bad Wolf? • Zip-A-Dee-Doo-Dah.
00100397...$6.95

26. Holly Season
21 favorite Christmas songs, including: Frosty the Snowman • I Heard the Bells on Christmas Day • Jingle-Bell Rock • O Holy Night • The Twelve Days of Christmas • We Wish You a Merry Christmas • The Christmas Waltz • My Favorite Things • Pretty Paper • Parade of the Wooden Soldiers.
00100100...$5.95

27. 60 of the World's Easiest to Play Songs with 3 Chords
Amazing Grace • Can-Can • Chopsticks • For He's a Jolly Good Fellow • Just a Closer Walk with Thee • Ode to Joy • Oh, Susanna • Yellow Rose of Texas • and more.
00001236...$7.95

28. 50 Classical Themes
50 familiar pieces, including: Beethoven Symphony No. 6 (5th Movement) • Eine Kleine Nachtmusik (4th Movement) • The Great Gate of Kiev (From "Pictures at an Exhibition") • Largo (From "Xerxes") • Meditation (From "Thais") • Mendelssohn Violin Concerto (1st Movement) • Mozart Piano Sonata in A (3rd Movement) • Song of India (From "Sadko") • Tchaikovsky Violin Concerto (1st Movement) • "William Tell" Overture (Closing Theme).
00101598...$9.95

29. Love Songs – Revised
Contains 24 popular love songs, including: Can You Feel the Love Tonight • The Glory of Love • The Look of Love • My Devotion • Shadows in the Moonlight • Try to Remember • Unforgettable • and more.
00100135...$6.95

30. Country Connection
20 country greats, including: Cool Water • Here I Am Drunk Again • I Don't Care • I Walk the Line • Love Me Tender • Release Me • Room Full of Roses • Since I Met You Baby • Wooden Heart.
00100030...$8.95

31. Big Band Favorites
21 all-time big band hits, including: East of the Sun • In a Little Spanish Town • I'll Remember April • It's the Talk of the Town • Manhattan • My Melancholy Baby • Pennies from Heaven • A String of Pearls • Tuxedo Junction • Yes, Indeed.
00100010...$6.95

32. Sing-Along Favorites
26 fun-to-play favorites: Let Me Call You Sweetheart • My Gal Sal • Down by the Old Mill Stream • Auld Lang Syne • Take Me Out to the Ball Game • and more.
00001289...$5.95

33. Memorable Standards
20 sentimental songs, including: Calcutta • Can't Help Falling in Love • Daddy's Little Girl • 'Deed I Do • Five Foot Two, Eyes of Blue • Let's Dance • Mr. Wonderful • Second-Hand Rose • That's All • Young at Heart.
00100150...$5.95

34. The Best of Reba McEntire
A perfect souvenir collection of 20 of Reba's favorite songs. Song highlights include: Only in My Mind • Somebody Should Leave • What Am I Gonna Do About You • Whoever's in New England • Sunday Kind of Love • You Lie • and more.
00102220...$8.95

35. Disney's Hercules
9 selections from the movie, including: Go the Distance • The Gospel Truth • I Won't Say (I'm in Love) • Zero to Hero • and more. Includes beautiful full-color art from the movie, too!
00100047...$12.95

37. Favorite Latin Songs
21 south-of-the-border standards, including: Amapola • C'est Si Bon • Chiapanecas • Cielito Lindo • Desafinado • Fascination • Guadalajara • Maria Elena • Meditation • El Reloj • Tango of Roses • more.
00100410...$5.95

38. Songs of the '90s
40 hot favorites, including: All For Love • Always • Beautiful in My Eyes • Colors of the Wind • Have I Told You Lately • Hold My Hand • Losing My Religion • The Power of Love • The River of Dreams • Save the Best for Last • The Sign • Tears in Heaven • Vision of Love • With One Look • and more.
00100032...$12.95

39. Songs of the '20s
21 favorites, including: April Showers • The Birth of the Blues • Charleston • I Know That You Know • I Want to Be Happy • Sometimes I'm Happy • Stout-Hearted Men • Sweet Georgia Brown • Tea for Two • Tip Toe Thru' the Tulips With Me.
00100580...$6.95

40. Songs of the '30s
Includes: April in Paris • Cheek to Cheek • Dancing on the Ceiling • Heart and Soul • I Found a Million Dollar Baby • Blue Hawaii • The Very Thought of You • Isn't It Romantic? • and more.
00100581...$7.95

41. Songs of Gershwin, Porter, & Rodgers
21 songs from these great composers, including: Anything Goes • The Blue Room • But Not for Me • Embraceable You • Fascinating Rhythm • I Got Rhythm • Oh! Lady Be Good • Somebody Loves Me • Thou Swell • What Is This Thing Called Love?
00100425...$6.95

43. Singalong Requests
21 singalongs, including: Ain't She Sweet • Ain't We Got Fun • Baby Face • Bye Bye Blackbird • California, Here I Come • Happy Days Are Here Again • I'm Looking Over a Four Leaf Clover • Moonlight Bay • My Heart Stood Still • Pretty Baby • Smiles.
00100576...$5.95

44. The Best of Willie Nelson
25 of his very best, including: Always on My Mind • Blue Eyes Crying in the Rain • Crazy • Georgia on My Mind • Help Me Make It Through the Night • Make the World Go Away • Mammas Don't Let Your Babies Grow Up to Be Cowboys • On the Road Again • To All the Girls I've Loved Before • and more.
00102135...$7.95

45. Love Ballads
Double Note Melodies
25 love songs, including: Canadian Sunset • Can't Help Lovin' Dat Man • I Will Wait for You • If I Loved You • The Last Time I Saw Paris • Little Girl Blue • Look for the Silver Lining • Lovely to Look At • Ol' Man River • This Can't Be Love • You'll Never Walk Alone.
00100460...$6.95

46. Hawaiian Favorites
21 favorites, including: Beyond the Reef • Ka-Lu-A • Lovely Hula Hands • Mapuana • Mele Kalikimaka • One Paddle-Two Paddle • The Sands of Waikiki • Songs of the Islands • That's the Hawaiian in Me • Waikiki.
00100090...$6.95

47. The Songs of Duke Ellington
22 of Duke Ellington's greatest songs, including: Don't Get Around Much Anymore • In a Sentimental Mood • It Don't Mean a Thing (If It Ain't Got That Swing) • Mood Indigo • Satin Doll • Sophisticated Lady • and more.
00100007...$8.95

48. Gospel Songs of Johnny Cash
20 songs, including: The Great Speckled Bird • Peace in the Valley • My God Is Real • On the Jericho Road • How Great Thou Art • The Old Rugged Cross • I'll Fly Away • Will the Circle Be Unbroken • Were You There When They Crucified My Lord? • Just a Closer Walk with Thee.
00100343...$5.95

49. Elvis, Elvis, Elvis
28 famous Elvis hits, including: All Shook Up • Blue Suede Shoes • Can't Help Falling in Love • Don't • Don't Be Cruel • Heartbreak Hotel • Hound Dog • It's Now or Never • Jailhouse Rock • Love Me Tender • (Let Me Be Your) Teddy Bear.
00100043...$8.95

50. The Best of Patsy Cline
24 of her best, including: Back in Baby's Arms • I Fall to Pieces • Three Cigarettes in an Ashtray • Your Cheatin' Heart • Crazy • and more.
00102114...$9.95

51. Sandi Patty Anthology
39 of her best, including: How Majestic Is Your Name • It's Your Song, Lord • Let There Be Praise • Love in Any Language • Make His Praise Glorious • More Than Wonderful • O Magnify the Lord • and more. Also includes a biography and photos of this inspirational singer.
00102121...$14.95

52. Top Country Hits of 1995-1996
21 hot hits, including: The Beaches of Cheyenne • It Matters to Me • The Keeper of the Stars • No News • One Boy, One Girl • Pickup Man • Tell Me I Was Dreaming • Texas Tornado • When You Say Nothing At All • Wild Angels • and more.
00100031 ....$10.95

53. Great American Composers: Stephen Foster
23 favorites in the American tradition, including: Camp-town Races • My Old Kentucky Home • Oh! Susanna • Old Black Joe • and more.
00001546 ....$5.95

54. Gospel Favorites
28 songs of inspiration, including: Amazing Grace • The Broken Vessel • He's Everything to Me • His Name Is Wonderful • I Asked the Lord • I've Just Seen Jesus • Just a Closer Walk with Thee • Lamb of Glory • Somebody Bigger Than You and I • To You I Give the Power • and more.
00100431 ....$6.95

55. Johnny Cash
28 songs, including: Folsom Prison Blues • I Walk the Line • Five Feet High and Rising • Don't Take Your Guns to Town • Daddy Sang Bass • Ragged Old Flag • San Quentin • Orange Blossom Special • Long Black Veil • Ring of Fire • John Henry • One Piece at a Time • many more.
00100342 ....$6.95

58. The Best of Lenny Dee
A collection of 16 recorded hits, including: Alabamy Bound • Alley Cat Song • By the Time I Get to Phoenix • Bye Bye Blues • The Exodus Song • Georgia on My Mind • Georgy Girl • Red Roses for a Blue Lady • Way Down Yonder in New Orleans • Yes, Sir, That's My Baby.
00100329 ....$5.95

59. Christmas Songs
22 songs, including: A Holly, Jolly Christmas • Home for the Holidays • I Heard the Bells on Christmas Day • I'll Be Home for Christmas • Let It Snow! Let It Snow! Let It Snow! • A Marshmallow World • Rockin' Around the Christmas Tree • Rudolph, the Red-Nosed Reindeer • Sleigh Ride • There Is No Christmas Like a Home Christmas.
00100353 ....$6.95

60. The Best of Eric Clapton
An excellent collection of 25 classics, including: Cocaine • Crossroads • I Shot the Sheriff • Layla • Sunshine of Your Love • Tears in Heaven • Wonderful Tonight • and more.
00102282 ....$9.95

61. Jazz Standards
Over 40 of the finest jazz songs ever, featuring: All of You • April in Paris • Autumn in New York • Body and Soul • Caravan • In the Wee Small Hours of the Morning • Mona Lisa • Mood Indigo • Satin Doll • Tangerine • The Very Thought of You • more.
00102314 ....$10.95

62. Favorite Hymns – Double Note Melodies
21 well-known hymns, including: Ave Maria • Bringing in the Sheaves • Come, Thou Almighty King • God of Our Fathers • Holy, Holy, Holy • Jesus Loves Me! This I Know • A Mighty Fortress Is Our God • My Faith Looks Up to Thee • The Old 100th Psalm • The Rosary • Stand Up! Stand Up for Jesus.
00100409 ....$5.95

63. Classical Music (English/Spanish Text)
22 classics: Barcarolle • Clair de Lune • Czardas • Dance of the Hours • Danube Waves • Fifth Symphony • Hungarian Dance No. 5 • Melody in F • Military Polonaise • Tannhauser March • Toccata and Fugue in D Minor • Waltz in A Minor.
00100360 ....$5.95

64. Christmas Cheer
19 holiday favorites: A Holly Jolly Christmas • The Little Drummer Boy • Merry Christ-mas, Darling • Silver and Gold • Silver Bells • Sleigh Ride • and more.
00001311 ....$5.95

65. Best of The Judds
15 of their best, including: Don't Be Cruel • Grandpa (Tell Me 'Bout the Good Old Days) • Rockin' with the Rhythm of the Rain • Why Not Me.
00101722 ....$5.95

66. Torch Songs
Sing your heart out with this collection of over 50 sultry jazz and big band melancholy masterpieces, including: Bewitched • Cry Me a River • Don't Explain • I Can't Get Started with You • I Got It Bad and That Ain't Good • Lover Man • Misty • My Funny Valentine • My One and Only Love • Stormy Weather • and many more.
00102312 ....$14.95

67. International Hits
21 world-renowned favorites, including: Esperanza • The Exodus Song • Für Elise • La Paloma • La Violetera • Los Nardos • Only You • Pequeña Flor • Valencia • more.
00100447 International Hits $5.95
00100666 Éxitos (Spanish Text) $5.95

68. Willie Nelson
21 songs, including: After the Fire Is Gone • Blue Eyes Crying in the Rain • Both Ends of the Candle • Congratulations • Country Willie • Crazy • Healing Hands of Time • I Gotta Get Drunk • Kneel at the Feet of Jesus • One Day at a Time.
00100250 ....$5.95

69. It's Gospel
27 songs, including: The Church in the Wildwood • Invisible Hands • It Took a Miracle • Mansion over the Hilltop • My God Is Real • Sweet, Sweet Song of Salvation • Take My Hand, Precious Lord • There'll Be Peace in the Valley for Me • Will the Circle Be Unbroken.
00100449 ....$6.95

70. Gospel Greats
26 gospel favorites, including: Beyond the Sunset • A Joyful Noise • In the Garden • It Is Well with My Soul • To God Be the Glory • Why Me? • He • Through It All • Holy Ground • Fully Alive • and more.
00100432 ....$6.95

71. Viennese Waltzes
21 songs, including: Danube Nymphs Waltz • Gold and Silver Waltz • The Merry Widow Waltz • Philomel Waltz • The Sirens • Sylvia • Tres Jolie (Charming Waltz) • Vienna Beauties • Village Swallows Waltz • Waltz, Op. 101, No. 11.
00100595 ....$5.95

74. Hymns of Glory
21 hymns, including: Break Thou the Bread of Life • Built on a Rock the Church Doth Stand • The Church's One Foundation • He Leadeth Me, O' Blessed Thought • I Need Thee Every Hour • Leaning on the Everlasting Arms • O Worship the King, All Glorious Above • Standing on the Promises.
00100444 ....$5.95

75. Sacred Moments
30 songs, including: I Love to Tell the Story • Love Lifted Me • Oh, How I Love Jesus • On Christ, the Solid Rock, I Stand • Send the Light • Tell Me the Old, Old Story • There Is Power in the Blood • 'Tis So Sweet to Trust in Jesus.
00100568 ....$6.95

76. The Sound of Music
Seven selections from the Broadway musical, including: Climb Ev'ry Mountain • Do-Re-Mi • Edelweiss • Maria • My Favorite Things • Sixteen Going on Seventeen • The Sound of Music.
00100572 ....$6.95

77. My Fair Lady
Seven selections from the Broadway musical: Get Me to the Church on Time • I Could Have Danced All Night • I've Grown Accustomed to Her Face • On the Street Where You Live • With a Little Bit of Luck • Wouldn't It Be Loverly.
00100489 ....$5.95

78. Oklahoma!
Seven selections from the Broadway musical: I Cain't Say No! • Many a New Day • Oh, What a Beautiful Mornin' • Oklahoma • Out Of My Dreams • People Will Say We're in Love • The Surrey With the Fringe on Top.
00100530 ....$5.95

79. South Pacific
7 selections from the Broadway musical: A Wonderful Guy • Bali Ha'i • Happy Talk • I'm Gonna Wash That Man Right Outa My Hair • Some Enchanted Evening • There Is Nothing Like a Dame • Younger than Springtime.
00100575 ....$5.95

80. The King and I
Seven selections from the Broadway musical: Getting to Know You • Hello, Young Lovers • I Have Dreamed • I Whistle a Happy Tune • Shall We Dance? • Something Wonderful • We Kiss in a Shadow.
00100456 ....$5.95

81. Frankie Yankovic Polkas & Waltzes
15 songs, including: Beer Barrel Polka • Bye Bye My Baby • Dance, Dance, Dance • Hoop-Dee-Doo • Just Another Polka • Pennsylvania Polka • Three Yanks Polka • The "Whoop" Polka • You Are My One True Love.
00100424 ....$5.95

82. Romantic Ballads & One Waltz
28 of the best, including: Don't Take Your Love from Me • I Can't Get Started with You • I'm Confessin' • It's the Talk of the Town • Seems Like Old Times • Smoke Gets in Your Eyes • This Love of Mine • Wonderful Copenhagen.
00100565..$7.95

83. Swingtime
26 swing standards, including: All of Me • Cry Me a River • Imagination • The Lady Is a Tramp • Let's Fall in Love • Lullaby of the Leaves • Moonlight in Vermont • Swinging on a Star • These Foolish Things Remind Me of You.
00100584..$6.95

84. Ballroom Favorites
25 danceable hits, including: Boo-Hoo • Cecilia • Charley My Boy • Love Walked In • Me and My Shadow • On a Slow Boat to China • Personality • Rags to Riches • Rockin' Chair • Then I'll Be Happy.
00100310..$6.95

85. Opera at the Movies
24 operatic favorites from movies like "Amadeus," "Apocalypse Now," "Breaking Away," "Chariots of Fire," "Fatal Attraction," "Godfather III," "Moonstruck," "Pretty Woman," and more.
00102315..$7.95

86. Songs from Musicals
21 of the best, including: Anywhere I Wander • Heart • Hernando's Hideaway • Hey There • If I Were a Bell • Once in Love with Amy • Seventy-Six Trombones • Stranger in Paradise • Till There Was You.
00100579..$5.95

87. The Beatles Best
More than 120 classics, including: All My Loving • And I Love Her • Blackbird • Come Together • Eleanor Rigby • Get Back • Help! • Hey Jude • Let It Be • Michelle • Sgt. Pepper's Lonely Hearts Club Band • She Loves You • Twist and Shout • Yesterday • many more.
00100313..$22.95

88. The Best of Roger Miller
A compilation of 20 of his best, including: Don't We All Have the Right • King of the Road • The Last Word in Lonesome Is Me • Walkin', Talkin', Cryin', Barely Beatin' Heart • You Can't Roller Skate in a Buffalo Herd • and more.
00102316..$8.95

89. Songs for Children
31 favorites, including: Are You Sleeping • Baa, Baa Black Sheep • Blow the Man Down • Chopsticks • The Farmer in the Dell • Hickory Dickory Dock • It Ain't Gonna Rain No More • London Bridge • Mulberry Bush • Row, Row, Row Your Boat • This Old Man.
00100577..$6.95

90. Elton John Anthology
60 of his greatest , including: Bennie and the Jets • Crocodile Rock • Daniel • Goodbye Yellow Brick Road • I Guess That's Why They Call It the Blues • Philadelphia Freedom • Rocket Man • Sad Songs (Say So Much) • Your Song.
00290104..$12.95

91. 30 Songs for a Better World
30 encouraging songs, including: Bless the Beasts and the Childen • Colors of the Wind • Everything Is Beautiful • From a Distance • If I Had a Hammer • Imagine • Love Can Build a Bridge • What a Wonderful World • and more.
00100034..$8.95

92. Familiar Hymns
22 favorites, including: Abide, O Dearest Jesus • All Glory and Honor • Draw Us to Thee • God Bless Our Native Land • Guide Me, O Thou Great Jehovah • Holy Ghost, with Light Divine • I Thou But Suffer God to Guide Thee • Jesus Sinners Doth Receive • O God, Thou Faithful God • Take My Life and Let It Be Consecrated.
00100411..$5.95

93. Country Hits
44 songs, including: All the Gold in California • Gentle on My Mind • I.O.U. • Lucille • Mammas, Don't Let Your Babies Grow Up to Be Cowboys • The Most Beautiful Girl • Sail Away • and more.
00100036..$9.95

95. Julio Iglesias
16 of his best, including: A Veces Tú, A Veces Yo • Abrázame • Cantándole Al Mar • Chiquilla • Como El Alamo Al Camino • Cuando Vuelva A Amanecer • Déjala • Desde Que Tú Te Has Ido • Diéciseis Años.
00100451 Spanish Text $6.95

96. Love Songs from the Movies
36 love songs from the silver screen, including: All for Love • Almost Paradise • Do You Know Where You're Going To? • Endless Love • Hopelessly Devoted to You • A Man and a Woman • Somewhere Out There • Tears in Heaven • and more.
00100044..$9.95

97. Elvis Presley's Songs of Inspiration
A collection of 33 well-known gospel songs recorded and interpreted by Elvis. Includes: Peace in the Valley • Take My Hand, Precious Lord • How Great Thou Art • Crying in the Chapel • Amazing Grace • and many more.
00102317..$9.95

98. Stage & Screen
21 greats, including: Hello, Young Lovers • I Enjoy Being a Girl • Love, Look Away • A Fellow Needs a Girl • No Other Love • People Will Say We're in Love • A Wonderful Guy • There's Nothing Like a Dame • We Kiss in a Shadow • You Are Beautiful.
00101950..$6.95

100. Winter Wonderland
15 all-time favorites, including: All I Want for Christmas Is My Two Front Teeth • Auld Lang Syne • Deck the Hall • Joy to the World • The Only Thing I Want for Christmas • What Did I Say to Old St. Nick? • When It's Christmas on the Range • Winter Wonderland.
00100602..$5.95

101. Annie
14 songs from the Broadway musical, including the hits: Easy Street • It's the Hard-Knock Life • Tomorrow • You're Never Fully Dressed Without a Smile • and more.
00100000..$5.95

102. The Carols of Christmas
24 sonLgs of the season, including: Joy to the World • O Come, O Come Immanuel • O Holy Night • Silent Night • and more.
00001309..$5.95

104. Bob Ralston – Broadway Memories
17 of Bob's all-time favorites, including: The Best Things in Life Are Free • Bewitched • Edelweiss • Getting to Know You • It Might As Well Be Spring • People Will Say We're in Love • The Surrey with the Fringe on Top.
00101544..$5.95

105. Best of Today's Movie Hits
19 recent hits, including: Change the World • Colors of the Wind • Cruella De Vil • Don't Cry for Me Argentina • The Dreame • Mission: Impossible Theme • Theme from Schindler's List • That Thing You Do! • and more.
00100039..$7.95

106. Barbra Streisand – Memories
10 great songs from the LP: Coming in and Out of Your Life • Evergreen • Lost Inside of You • The Love Inside • Memory • My Heart Belongs to Me • New York State of Mind • No More Tears • The Way We Were • You Don't Bring Me Flowers.
00101958..$6.95

107. The Best of Bob Ralston
21 favorites, including: All The Things You Are • Have You Ever Been Lonely • If Ever I Would Leave You • I Left My Heart in San Francisco • My Prayer • Twilight Time • Watch What Happens • When My Baby Smiles at Me • World Is Waiting for the Sunrise • Yesterdays.
00101515..$5.95

108. Classical Themes (English/Spanish Text)
18 favorites, including: Ave Maria • Barcarole • Für Elise • Hallelujah Chorus • Jesu, Joy of Man's Desiring • Liebestraum • Minuet in G • Moonlight Sonata • Theme from Swan Lake • Unfinished Symphony.
00100363..$6.95

109. Motown's Greatest Hits
43 of Motown's biggest hits, including: ABC • Ain't No Mountain High Enough • Baby Love • Dancing in the Street • For Once in My Life • Heatwave • I Heard It Through the Grapevine • Just My Imagination • My Guy • Shop Around • You Keep Me Hangin' On • and more.
00102232..$12.95

110. The Neil Diamond Collection
44 of his best, including: America • Cracklin' Rose • Forever in Blue Jeans • Heartlight • Hello Again • Longfellow Serenade • Love on the Rocks • September Morn • Song Sung Blue • Sweet Caroline • Yesterday's Songs • You Don't Bring Me Flowers.
00101566..$9.95

112. The Best of The Beatles
200 pages and 89 songs, including: All My Loving • Day Tripper • Penny Lane • And I Love Her • Eight Days a Week • A Hard Days Night • Help! • Norwegian Wood • Michelle • Ticket to Ride • Yesterday • Eleanor Rigby • Yellow Submarine • When I'm Sixty-Four • Hey Jude • Let It Be.
00101498...$16.95

114. Country Treasures
27 favorites, including: Don't It Make Your Brown Eyes Blue • Don't Fall in Love With a Dreamer • God Bless the U.S.A. • It's Hard to Be Humble • Somebody's Knocking • You Decorated My Life • and many more.
00101228...$7.95

115. The Greatest Waltzes
37 waltzes, including: Allegheny Moon • The Blue Skirt Waltz • Edelweiss • Falling in Love with Love • Fascination • I'll Take Romance • It's a Grand Night for Singing • Let Me Call You Sweetheart • Melody of Love • My Favorite Things • Oh, What a Beautiful Mornin' • Tennessee Waltz • True Love • Wunderbar • You Can't Be True Dear.
00101612...$8.95

116. Don Ho Songbook
30 favorites, including: Aloha • The Far Lands • Hawaiian Guitar • Here Is Happiness • Keanani • Luau Song • Mau'i Waltz • Moya • My Lovely Lei • Our Love and Aloha • Pearly Shells • Puka Shells • Tania • This Is Paradise • Tiny Bubbles.
00100407...$6.95

117. Willie Nelson – Just Plain Willie
37 songs, including 28 unreleased songs plus these 9 bonus tracks: Always on My Mind • Blue Eyes Crying in the Rain • Crazy • I'm Gonna Sit Right Down and Write Myself a Letter • Mammas Don't Let Your Babies Grow Up to Be Cowboys • My Heroes Have Always Been Cowboys • Star Dust • Up Against the Wall Red-Neck • Without a Song.
00101725...$7.95

119. 57 Super Hits
57 top tunes like: Autumn Leaves • The Christmas Song • Dinah • Enjoy Yourself • Five Minutes More • Hello, Dolly! • Mister Sandman • One • Peggy Sue • Put on a Happy Face • Real Live Girl • Sentimental Journey • S'posin' • Tenderly • Vaya Con Dios • and many more.
00101990...$12.95

120. The Gospel Songs of Bill and Gloria Gaither
67 favorites in all, including: Abide in Me • Because He Lives • Get All Excited • He Touched Me • I Walked Today Where Jesus Walks • I've Been to Calvary • Jesus, I Believe What You Said • Precious Jesus • The Family of God • Next Time We Meet • This Is the Day That the Lord Hath Made • Upon This Rock.
00100433...$12.95

121. Boogies, Blues & Rags
20 greats, including: Basin Street Blues • Bugle Call Rag • A Good Man Is Hard to Find • King Porter Stomp • The Man That Got Away • Maple Leaf Rag • The Original Boogie Woogie • Pine Top's Boogie • Stormy Weather • Sugar Foot Stomp.
00100333...$5.95

123. 58 Super Hits
Includes: The Best Things in Life Are Free • Bewitched • Candy • Carioca • Dream a Little Dream of Me • A Foggy Day • How High the Moon • I Love Paris • Lilli Marlene • Mood Indigo • Old Devil Moon • Small World • Sugar Blues • That's Entertainment • That's Life • The Way You Look Tonight • Who? • and many more.
00101991...$12.95

124. Country Christmas
26 favorites, including: Blue Christmas • Christmas California • Didn't He Shine • Hard Candy Christmas • It's Christmas • Little One • Old Toy Trains • Pretty Paper • Tennessee Christmas.
00101559...$5.95

125. The Great Big Book of Children's Songs
73 of the best children's songs ever, including: A Whole New World • Are You Sleeping • Candy Man • Cruella De Vil • Heart and Soul • House at Pooh Corner • Kum Ba Yah • Puff the Magic Dragon • Sing •Won't You Be My Neighbor? • Candy Man • and more.
00100001...$12.95

126. Best of Barry Manilow
24 of his best, including: Can't Smile Without You • Copacabana • I Made it Through the Rain • I Write the Songs • Mandy • This One's for You • Tryin' to Get the Feeling Again • Weekend in New England.
00101497...$9.95

127. John Denver's Greatest Hits
23 of his greatest, including: Annie's Song • Back Home Again • My Sweet Lady • Rocky Mountain High • Sunshine on My Shoulders • more.
00101563...$8.95

128. Neil Diamond's Greatest Hits
19 songs, including: Beautiful Noise • Forever in Blue Jeans • I Am, I Said • Kentucky Woman • Play Me • Rosemary's Wine • Shilo • Solitary Man • Soolaimon • Sweet Caroline • You Don't Bring Me Flowers.
00100394...$6.95

129. The Groovy Years
Bring out your bell bottoms and get down with 42 favorites, including: All You Need Is Love • Born to Be Wild • California Dreamin' • Everybody's Talkin' • For Your Love • Groovin' • Happy Together • Helter Skelter • Leaving on a Jet Plane • Me and Bobby McGee • Nights in White Satin • Revolution • San Francisco (Be Sure Wear Some Flowers in Your Hair) • Spinning Wheel • Turn! Turn! Turn! • Wild Thing • and more. Includes an interesting time capsule of photos and writings from the era.
00100037...$10.95

130. Rock 'N' Roll Is Here to Stay
26 songs, including: Back in the U.S.A. • Bo Diddley • Great Balls of Fire • Johnny B. Goode • Long Tall Sally • Mabelline • Rip It Up • Rock & Roll Music • Roll over Beethoven • Shake, Rattle and Roll • Sh-Boom • Silhouettes • Stagger Lee • Surfin' U.S.A.
00100563...$7.95

131. The Doo-Wop Songbook
40 favorites from yesteryear, featuring: Book of Love • Doo Wah Diddy Diddy • Duke of Earl • Goodnight, Sweetheart, Goodnight (Goodnight It's Time to Go) • Sixteen Candles • Stay • This Magic Moment • and more.
00102318...$10.95

132. Songs of Love
24 songs, including: Anniversary Song • Bridal Chorus • Could I Have This Dance • Endless Love • I Love You Truly • If I Loved You • Let Me Call You Sweetheart • True Love • Wedding March • When I Fall in Love • You Needed Me.
00101944...$5.95

134. That Christmas Feeling
22 holiday favorites, including: Christmas Is • The Christmas Song • Frosty the Snow Man • It's Beginning to Look Like Christmas • Jingle-Bell Rock • Nuttin' for Christmas • Silver Bells • We Need a Little Christmas • and many more.
00100586...$6.95

135. Reba – For My Broken Heart
Matching folio to the album, featuring: The Greatest Man I Never Knew • Is There Life Out There • The Night the Lights Went Out in Georgia • and more.
00102285...$6.95

136. Christmas Is for Kids
18 easy children's favorites: A Holly Jolly Christmas • Go Tell It on the Mountain • Rockin' Around the Christmas Tree • and more. Also includes coloring pages and puzzles.
00001256...$6.95

138. Nostalgia Collection
100 songs from the good ol' days, complete with interesting historical notes on each piece. Songs include: Aba Daba Honeymoon • Aloha Oe • Anchors Aweigh • Beale Street Blues • The Bells of St. Mary's • By the Light of the Silvery Moon • The Entertainer • The Glow Worm • How 'Ya Gonna Keep 'Em Down on the Farm? • I Wonder Who's Kissing Her Now? • Let Me Call You Sweetheart • The Merry Widow Waltz • Pretty Baby • Shine On, Harvest Moon • St. Louis Blues • Swanee • Take Me Out to the Ball Game • You Made Me Love You • and more!
00100038...$14.95

139. The Best of Jerome Kern
27 great melodies, including: All the Things You Are • Can't Help Lovin' Dat Man • The Last Time I Saw Paris • Look for the Silver Lining • Ol' Man River • Smoke Gets in Your Eyes • Why Do I Love You?
00101732...$7.95

140. The Best of George Strait – 2nd Edition
A collection of 33 of his best, updated to include his latest hits: All My Ex's Live in Texas • Baby's Gotten Good at Goodbye • Blue Clear Sky • Does Fort Worth Ever Cross Your Mind • I've Come to Expect It from You • Love Without End, Amen • and more.
00101956...$12.95

141. All-Time Latin Favorites
17 songs, including: Call Me • The Girl from Ipanema • Green Eyes • My Shawl • One Note Samba • Perhaps, Perhaps, Perhaps • Poinciana • Return to Me • So Nice (Summer Samba) • Yellow Bird.
00100290..$5.95

142. 59 Super Hits
Features: Allegheny Moon • Boogie Woogie Bugle Boy • Early Autumn • For All We Know • I'll Take Romance • It's Only a Paper Moon • Little Girl • Love Is a Simple Thing • Memories • People • She • Stay With Me • Swedish Rhapsody • Unchained Melody • When Irish Eyes Are Smiling • Willow Weep for Me • Yearning • more!
00101992..$12.95

143. Movie Musical Memories
Over 30 great songs from movie musicals, including: Anniversary Song • Isn't It Romantic • Long Ago (And Far Away) • Moonlight Becomes You • Over the Rainbow • Puttin' on the Ritz • Singin' in the Rain • The Way You Look Tonight • and more.
00100003..$10.95

144. All-Time TV Favorites
Over 65 great themes from TV shows like: The Flintstones • Andy Griffith • Batman • The Dick Van Dyke Show • Hawaii Five-O • Jeopardy • Love American Style • Northern Exposure • The Odd Couple • Fraiser • and more.
00100013..$17.95

145. It's Love – 2nd Edition
15 love songs, including: Can You Feel the Love Tonight? • Don't Know Much • Endless Love • Just the Way You Are • The Keeper of the Stars • Save the Best for Last • Somewhere Out There • When I Fall in Love • and more.
00001294..$6.95

146. Hank Williams – His Best
26 of his biggest, including: Cold, Cold Heart • Countryfied • Hey, Good Lookin' • Honky Tonk Blues • I Can't Help It (If I'm Still in Love With You) • I Saw the Light • I'm So Lonesome I Could Cry • Jambalaya (On the Bayou) • Kaw-Liga • Mansion on the Hill • My Son Calls Another Man Daddy • Ramblin' Man • You Win Again • Your Cheatin' Heart.
00100597..$7.95

147. Folk Songs of England, Scotland & Ireland
44 folk favorites, including: The Foggy, Foggy Dew • John Peel • Lincolnshire Poacher • The Vicar of Bray • The Blue Bells of Scotland • Bonny Mary of Argyle • Lock Lomond • My Love Is Like a Red Red Rose • Scotland the Brave • Wi' a Hundred Pipers • Come Back to Erin • The Dear Little Shamrock • The Wearin' O' the Green.
00100420..$6.95

148. Barbra Streisand – One Voice
Matching folio to this smash LP from Streisand – her first live performance in twenty years. 12 songs, including: Evergreen • It's a New World • Over the Rainbow • Papa, Can You Hear Me? • People • Somewhere • The Way We Were.
00101960..$6.95

149. "Endless Love" & Other Great Love Songs
32 greats, including: Coming In and Out of Your Life • Endless Love • Falling in Love with Love • Feelings • If This Isn't Love • Love Is Here to Stay • Loving You • Melody of Love • My Funny Valentine • Nevertheless • September Morn • So in Love • Till • Till We Two Are One.
00100406..$6.95

150. The Best Big Band Songs Ever
69 of the greatest big band songs of all time, including: Ballin' the Jack • Basin Street Blues • Boogie Woogie Bugle Boy • The Continental • Don't Get Around Much Anymore • In the Mood • Opus One • Satin Doll • Sentimental Journey • String of Pearls.
00101548..$15.95

153. Our God Reigns
30 spiritual favorites from contemporary Christian artists. Songs include: Bless His Holy Name • El Shaddai • Give Thanks • Great Is the Lord • Jesus Is the Answer • Our God Reigns • Say the Name • There Is Joy in the Lord • Thy Word • and more.
00100004..$10.95

155. The Best of Billy Joel
22 of his best, including: And So It Goes • Honesty • It's Still Rock and Roll To Me • Just the Way You Are • My Life • Piano Man • Uptown Girl • We Didn't Start the Fire • more!
00101549..$9.95

156. The Best of Rodgers & Hart
20 songs, including: Bewitched • Falling in Love With Love • Isn't It Romantic? • The Lady Is a Tramp • My Funny Valentine • There's a Small Hotel • and more.
00100033..$6.95

157. Easy Favorites
25 songs, including: When the Saints Go Marching In • Marianne • Londonderry Air • Greensleeves • and more.
00001264..$5.95

158. The John Lennon Collection
15 of his best, including: Give Peace a Chance • Imagine • Instant Karma • Mind Games • (Just Like) Starting Over • Watching the Wheels • Whatever Gets You Through the Night • Woman • and more.
00101769..$6.95

159. Cats
Ten songs from this spectacular show, including the award-winning "Memory," plus: Gus: The Theatre Cat • Jellicle Songs for Jellicle Cats • Mr. Mistoffelees • and more.
00101551..$8.95

160. 60 Super Hits
Features: Bandstand Boogie • Count Every Star • Daddy's Little Girl • Edelweiss • Five Foot Two, Eyes of Blue • Gigi • I'll Remember April • It Might As Well Be Spring • My Heart Belongs to Me • Never on Sunday • She Loves You • The Third Man Theme • Too Young • Where or When • Young at Heart • and more.
00101993..$12.95

161. 61 Super Hits
Features: Among My Souvenirs • Come Back to Me • The First Time Ever I Saw Your Face • From This Moment On • I Left My Heart in San Francisco • I'll Be Seeing You • If I Ruled the World • In the Still of the Night • Just in Time • My Funny Valentine • Old Cape Cod • A String of Pearls • Through the Years • many more.
00101994..$14.95

162. Lounge Music Collection
40 songs, including: Alfie • Born Free • (They Long to Be) Close to You • Copacabana (At the Copa) • Feelings • Fever • The Girl from Ipanema • Misty • Moon River • Satin Doll • The Way You Look Tonight • and more.
00100049..$9.95

163. R&B Ballads
30 songs, including: Ain't Nothing Like the Real Thing • Ben • Do You Know Where You're Going to? • Easy • I Second That Emotion • Just My Imagination • My Girl • Still • The Tracks of My Tears • What's Going On • Where Did Our Love Go • and more.
00100050..$8.95

164. The Best Christmas Songbook
30 all-time favorites, including: Coventry Carol • Deck the Halls • Frosty the Snowman • God Rest Ye, Merry Gentlemen • The Holly and the Ivy • I Saw Three Ships • Rudolph, the Red-Nosed Reindeer • Silent Night • We Wish You a Merry Christmas • Little Drummer Boy • more.
00101530..$7.95

165. The Rodgers & Hammerstein Songbook
37 excellent songs from these shows: Carousel • Flower Drum Song • The King and I • Me and Juliet • Oklahoma! • Pipe Dream • South Pacific • The Sound of Music • State Fair.
00101895..$8.95

166. The New Novelty Songbook
40 fun favorites, including: Alley-Oop • The Bunny Hop • Hello Mudduh, Hello Fadduh! • Itsy Bitsy Teenie Weenie Yellow Polka Dot Bikini • Purple People Eater • Rama Lama Ding Dong • Supercalifragilisticexpialidocious • Yakety Yak • and more.
00101809..$9.95

168. Barbra Streisand – The Broadway Album Songbook
All ten of the songs from the smash hit album, featuring: Can't Help Lovin' Dat Man • If I Loved You • Send in the Clowns • Something Wonderful • Somewhere • and more.
00101959..$6.95

170. Kenny Rogers Greatest Hits
16 of his best, including: Coward of the County • The Gambler • Love the World Away • Reuben James • Ruby • She Believes in Me • A Love Song.
00101900..$9.95

171. The Best of Elton John – 2nd Edition
16 songs, including: Can You Feel the Love Tonight • Candle in the Wind • Crocodile Rock • Daniel • Don't Let the Sun Go Down on Me • Goodbye Yellow Brick Road • Rocket Man • Someone Saved My Life Tonight • Sorry Seems to Be the Hardest Word • Your Song.
00101537..$6.95

172. The Music Man
Eight selections from the Broadway musical, featuring: Gary, Indiana • Seventy-Six Trombones • Till There Was You • Wells Fargo Wagon • and more.
00101796..$5.95

173. The New Complete Wedding Songbook
A wonderful collection of 45 classic pop and standard wedding songs: Just the Way You Are • Longer • The Lord's Prayer • Anniversary Song • Endless Love • Feelings • Love Me Tender • You Needed Me • and more.
00101558..$10.95

174. One for My Lady
50 great songs celebrating women made famous in song. Includes: Angie • Betty Boop • Gigi • Hello Mary Lou • Help Me Rhonda • If You Knew Susie • K-K-K Katy • Lilli Marlene • Maggie May • Mona Lisa • Peg O' My Heart • and more.
00100018..$14.95

175. Wedding Songs Country Style
29 country love songs, including: The Battle Hymn of Love • Could I Have This Dance • Forever and Ever, Amen • Grow Old With Me • The Keeper of the Stars • Long As I Live • Love Can Build a Bridge • Love Without End, Amen • Marry Me • Through the Years • The Vows Go Unbroken • and more.
00100052..$8.95

177. I'll Be Seeing You: 50 Songs of World War II
Ac-cent-tchu-ate the Positive • Don't Sit Under the Apple Tree • Ev'ry Time We Say Goodbye • I'll Be Home for Christmas • It's Been A Long, Long Time • Love Letters • Moonlight in Vermont • Sentimental Journey • You'll Never Know.
00100019..$12.95

178. "Jailhouse Rock," "Kansas City" & Other Hits of Lieber & Stoller
22 of their best, including the title tracks and: Bossa Nova Baby • Charlie Brown • Hound Dog • I'm a Woman • Love Potion Number 9 • On Broadway • Stand By Me • Yakety Yak • and more.
00100051..$8.95

179. Love Songs of The Beatles
21 of the Beatles' best ballads, including: And I Love Her • From Me to You • Hey Jude • If I Fell • In My Life • It's Only Love • Michelle • Something • Yesterday • and more.
00102325..$8.95

181. The Great American Country Songbook
70 songs, including: Any Day Now • By the Time I Get to Phoenix • Cold, Cold Heart • Daytime Friends • El Paso • Every Which Way But Loose • Heartbroke • I Don't Care • I Love • I Walk the Line • I Wouldn't Have Missed It for the World • It Was Almost Like a Song • It's a Heartache • It's Hard to Be Humble.
00101610..$12.95

182. Amazing Grace – 2nd Edition
A great collection of 100 inspirational favorites, including the title song and: Ave Maria • Beautiful Savior • Faith of Our Fathers • Go Down, Moses • Holy, Holy, Holy • I'll Live for Him • Jesus Loves Me • Rock of Ages • Tell Me the Old, Old Story • and more.
00001246..$12.95

183. 63 Super Hits
Features: Calcutta • Charmaine • Day by Day • 'Deed I Do • Fever • Green Door • Happy Together • Indiana • Lady • Love Will Keep Us Together • Memory • Midnight Blue • Mr. Mountain Rain • Somebody's Knockin' • Stand by Me • Stand by Your Man • Swingin' • Your Cheatin' Heart.
00101996..$14.95

184. Merle Haggard Anthology
A comprehensive collection of 47 of the best from country legend. Song highlights: From Graceland to the Promised Land • If We Make It Through December • Mama Tried • Okie from Muskogee • and many more.
00290252..$10.95

186. 40 Pop & Rock Song Classics
Features: Goodbye Girl • A Horse with No Name • Hotel California • The Hustle • Margaritaville • On Broadway • Rhinestone Cowboy • The Rose • Southern Nights • Take It to the Limit • Time in a Bottle • We Are Family.
00101606..$12.95

188. 64 Standard Hits
Features: God Bless' the Child • If Ever I Would Leave You • Islands in the Stream • Manhattan • Memory • More • Paper Doll • September Song • Song Sung Blue • Total Eclipse of the Heart • Try to Remember • What a Diff'rence a Day Made.
00101997..$14.95

189. Irish Favorites
Features 31 of the most popular Irish songs of all time, including: Danny Boy • Galway Piper • Has Anybody Here Seen Kelly • If I Knock the 'L' Out of Kelly • A Little Bit of Heaven • McNamara's Band • Molly Malone • and more.
00102276..$7.95

190. 17 Super Christmas Hits
Includes: The Christmas Waltz • Frosty the Snowman • I'll Be Home for Christmas • It's Beginning to Look Like Christmas • Rudolph, the Red-Nosed Reindeer • Sleigh Ride • We Need a Little Christmas.
00101939..$6.95

191. Jazz Love Songs
35 songs, including: All the Things You Are • Falling in Love with Love • A Fine Romance • I Don't Know Why (I Just Do) • Isn't It Romantic? • My Funny Valentine • Smoke Gets in Your Eyes • There's a Small Hotel • and more.
00100053..$7.95

192. 65 Standard Hits
Includes: Begin the Beguine • Brian's Song • Dancing in the Dark • Hooray for Hollywood • I Only Have Eyes for You • The Look of Love • Misty • New York, New York • Put Your Hand in the Hand • The Rose • Spanish Eyes • There's a Kind of Hush • Wonderland by Night • You Do Something to Me • and more.
00101998..$14.95

193. 66 Standard Hits
Features: Ain't She Sweet • Autumn in New York • Born Free • I Gotta Right to Sing the Blues • Just One of Those Things • L-O-V-E • Let's Fly Away • Liza • Theme from M*A*S*H • Near You • Night and Day • Nine to Five • Poor Butterfly • Skylark • Snowbird • Sweet Georgia Brown • What's New • and more.
00101999..$14.95

194. 67 Standard Hits
Includes: Always on My Mind • April in Paris • Bye Bye Blackbird • Dream • If • Java Jive • Jean • Lullaby of Broadway • Theme from Mahogany • The Man I Love • Nadia's Theme • Smiles • Strike Up the Band • Tea for Two • Time After Time • A Time for Love • What Is This Thing Called Love • more.
00101941..$15.95

195. Feel Good Fun
32 songs to make you smile, including: ABC • The Candy Man • Daydream Believer • Hang on Sloopy • I'm Henry VIII, I Am • Making Our Dreams Come True • Sugar, Sugar • and more.
00100054..$8.95

196. The Best of George Gershwin
27 great songs, including: A Foggy Day • Embraceable You • I Got Plenty O' Nuttin' • I Got Rhythm • I've Got a Crush on You • It Ain't Necessarily So • Let's Call the Whole Thing Off • Nice Work If You Can Get It • S' Wonderful • Shall We Dance • Summertime • They Can't Take That Away From Me.
00101609..$7.95

197. Acoustic Classics
Over 30 songs, including: American Pie • Angie • Blackbird • Dust in the Wind • Free Bird • Leaving on a Jet Plane • Longer • Maggie May • Rocky Mountain High • Turn! Turn! Turn! • You've Got a Friend • and more.
00100056..$9.95

198. Songs in 3/4 Time
49 melodic favorites, including many popular waltzes. Titles include: The Anniversary Waltz • Edelweiss • Fascination • I'll Take Romance • Moon River • Que Sera, Sera • The Rainbow Connection • Tenderly • Try to Remember • Wunderbar • and more.
00100057..$9.95

199. Jumbo Songbook
274 songs for all occasions: College Songs • Patriotic Songs • Humorous Songs • International Folk Songs • Classical Themes • Sacred Songs • Latin Songs • Polkas And Marches • Waltzes • Sing-alongs • Children's Songs • Christmas Carols • Wedding Music.
00100453..$19.95

200. Best Songs Ever – 4th Edition
80 of the very best songs ever, including: All I Ask of You • Blue Skies • Don't Cry for Me Argentina • Edelweiss • Endless Love • Girl from Ipanema • Have I Told You Lately • I Left My Heart in San Francisco • Love Me Tender • Memory • Satin Doll • Stardust • Tears in Heaven • A Time for Us • Unchained Melody • Unforgettable • When You Wish Upon a Star • Yesterday • and more.
00101539..$18.95

201. The Richard Clayderman Songbook
Thirteen hits, including: Ballade Pour Adeline • Feelings • Hello • Lara's Theme • Love Is Blue • Love Story • Memory • Moon River • more.
00101555..$5.95

202. The Best Country Songs Ever
Over 75 all-time favorites, including: Forever and Ever, Amen • Friends in Low Places • Love Without End, Amen • Always on My Mind • Behind Closed Doors • Crazy • D-I-V-O-R-C-E • God Bless the U.S.A. • Through the Years • more.
00101540..$17.95

203. The Best Broadway Songs Ever
74 of the all-time greatest Broadway hits, including: All I Ask of You • Don't Cry for Me Argentina • People • The Last Night of the World • Love Changes Everything • Memory • Send in the Clowns • Sunrise, Sunset • You'll Never Walk Alone. Features special stay-open binding.
00101541..$17.95

204. The Best Easy Listening Songs Ever
Over 70 favorites, including: All out of Love • Blue Velvet • Careless Whisper • Dust in the Wind • Every Breath You Take • Hey Jude • I Write the Songs • Lost in Your Eyes • Piano Man • The Rainbow Connection • Unchained Melody • Vision of Love • Your Song • and more.
00101542..$16.95

205. The Best Love Songs Ever
Over 60 sentimental favorites, including: Anniversary Song • (They Long to Be) Close to You • Don't Know Much • Endless Love • Just the Way You Are • Longer • Love Takes Time • Misty • My Funny Valentine • Sea of Love • Through the Years • You Needed Me • Your Song • and more.
00101543..$17.95

206. Favorite Children's Songs – Second Edition
31 fun favorites, including: A-Tisket A-Tasket • Alouette • Chim Chim Cher-ee • Edelweiss • Frosty the Snow Man • Hakuna Matata • The Rainbow Connection • Supercalifragilisticexpiali-docious • This Land Is Your Land • Won't You Be My Neighbor? • and more.
00101585..$6.95

207. Jim Henson's Muppets™
18 favorites, including: Mah-na, Mah-na • Movin' Right Along • Muppet Babies Theme • The Muppet Show Theme • Never Before, Never Again • The Rainbow Connection • and more.
00101698..$5.95

208. Easy Listening Favorites
24 songs, including: Always on My Mind • Bless the Beasts and Children • Cherish • I Write the Songs • Moon River • Nadia's Theme • Raindrops Keep Fallin' on My Head • Somewhere Out There • The Way We Were • and more.
00100058..$7.95

209. Disney Christmas Favorites
24 holiday favorites, including: Deck the Hall • Hark! The Herald Angels Sing • Jingle Bells • O Come All Ye Faithful • Silent Night • and more Christmas hits.
00101570..$6.95

210. '60s Pop/Rock
A great collection of 51 classics: Angel of the Morning • Blue Velvet • The Boy from New York City • Crying • Daydream Believer • Down-town • Love Me Do • Monday, Monday • Oh, Pretty Woman • Please Mr. Postman • Return to Sender • Twist and Shout • You Keep Me Hangin' On • and more.
00100059..$12.95

211. The Great Movie Musical Songbook
61 sensational songs from movie musicals. Includes: Cheek to Cheek • A Foggy Day • Funny Girl • Heat Wave • Just in Time • You Do Something to Me • more.
00100021..$14.95

213. The Big Book of Disney Songs
40 of Disney's best, including: Candle on the Water • A Dream Is a Wish Your Heart Makes • It's a Small World • Let's Go Fly a Kite • Mickey Mouse March • Some Day My Prince Will Come • A Spoonful of Sugar • Supercalifragilisticexpialidocious • When You Wish Upon a Star • Zip-A-Dee-Doo-Dah.
00101546..$21.95

214. Silver Bells
19 holiday favorites, including: Silver Bells • Do You Hear What I Hear? • The Most Wonderful Day of the Year • Sleigh Ride • more.
00001312..$5.95

215. The Best Christmas Songs Ever – 3rd Edition
79 holiday classics: Do You Hear What I Hear • Feliz Navidad • Frosty the Snow Man • Grandma Got Run Over by a Reindeer • Jingle-Bell Rock • Let It Snow! Let It Snow! Let It Snow! • Rudolph the Red-Nosed Reindeer • Silver Bells • and more!
00101533..$17.95

216. Still More Songs of the '80s
40 songs, including: Always • Don't You (Forget About Me) • Heat of the Moment • Here and Now • Jessie's Girl • Neutron Dance • Owner of a Lonely Heart • Sweet Dreams (Are Made of This) • True Blue • Woman in Love • and more.
00100060..$12.95

217. Movie Ballads
37 songs, including: Alfie • Beauty and the Beast • Born Free • Funny Girl • The Glory of Love • Isn't It Romantic? • Mona Lisa • Somewhere Out There • Three Coins in the Fountain • The Way We Were • When I Fall in Love • You Must Love Me • and more.
00100040..$8.95

218. I Will Praise Him
19 of the best-loved songs of devotion, including: Great Is the Lord • He's Alive • How Majestic Is Your Name • Lamb of God • O Magnify the Lord • Upon This Rock • and more.
00102213..$6.95

220. Wedding Songs of Love and Friendship
28 songs of devotion, including: Because • Doubly Good to You • I Am Loved • Longer • The Lord's Prayer • Portrait of Love • Sunrise, Sunset • What a Difference You've Made in My Life.
00102072..$7.95

221. The Randy Travis Songbook
20 of his greatest hits, including: Diggin' Up Bones • Forever and Ever, Amen • On the Other Hand • more.
00102035..$9.95

222. New Contemporary Country
24 hit country tunes, including: Always Late With Your Kisses • Famous Last Words of a Fool • I'll Still Be Loving You • Love Will Find Its Way to You • Ocean Front Property • Straight to the Heart • Turn It Loose.
00101557..$6.95

223. Glorious Praise
26 songs of worship and praise, including: Find a Way • Friends • How Excellent Is Thy Name • How Majestic Is Your Name • O Magnify the Lord • Via Dolorosa • more.
00101614..$6.95

224. Amy Grant's Greatest Hits
21 of this Christian superstar's best songs, including: Find a Way • Tennessee Christmas • Angels • El Shaddai • Doubly Good to You.
00101458..$7.95

225. The Lawrence Welk Songbook
51 great songs made famous by Lawrence Welk, including: Apples and Bananas • Bubbles in the Wine • Calcutta • Liechtensteiner Polka • Mack the Knife • The Poor People of Paris • The Wayward Wind • more.
00102080..$9.95

226. Award-Winning Songs of the Country Music Association – 3rd Edition
75 award-winning country classics, including: Achy Breaky Heart • Ain't That Lonely Yet • Always on My Mind • Boot Scootin' Boogie • Daddy's Hands • Forever and Ever, Amen • God Bless the U.S.A. • He Thinks He'll Keep Her • I Swear • I'm Not Lisa • Islands in the Stream • The Keeper of the Stars • Lucille • Ode to Billy Joe • Rhinestone Cowboy • She Believes in Me • Where've You Been • and more.
00101482..$16.95

228. Songs of the '20s
56 songs, including: Ain't Misbehavin' • Among My Souvenirs • Button Up Your Overcoat • 'Deed I Do • Everybody Loves My Baby • Five Foot Two, Eyes of Blue • Honeysuckle Rose • Look for the Silver Lining • Ol' Man River • When the Red, Red Robin Comes Bob, Bob Bobbin' Along • Yes! We Have No Bananas • and more.
00101931..$12.95

229. Songs of the '30s
58 songs, including: All of Me • A Foggy Day • In the Mood • My Funny Valentine • Pennies from Heaven • What a Diff'rence a Day Made • You're My Everything • and more.
00101932..$12.95

230. Songs of the '40s
62 songs, including: Anniversary Song • Come Rain or Come Shine • God Bless' the Child • How High the Moon • Old Devil Moon • People Will Say We're in Love • So in Love • A String of Pearls • The Things We Did Last Summer • You'd Be So Nice to Come Home To • and more.
00101933..$12.95

231. Songs of the '50s
60 songs, including: All I Have to Do Is Dream • Blue Suede Shoes • Blue Velvet • Crying in the Chapel • Here's That Rainy Day • Misty • The Party's Over • Shake, Rattle and Roll • They Call the Wind Maria • Unforgettable • Young at Heart • and more.
00101934..$13.95

232. Songs of the '60s
61 songs, including: As Long As He Needs Me • By the Time I Get to Phoenix • Dominique • The Girl from Ipanema • Hello Mary Lou • If I Had a Hammer • Love Is Blue • Monday, Monday • Our Day Will Come • Please, Please Me • That's Life • Those Were the Days • A Whiter Shade of Pale • and more.
00101935..$13.95

233. Songs of the '70s
49 songs, including: After the Love Has Gone • Daniel • Don't Cry for Me Argentina • Feelings • How Deep Is Your Love • Imagine • Joy to the World • Just the Way You Are • Laughter in the Rain • Let It Be • Mandy • Nights in White Satin • Send in the Clowns • Song Sung Blue • You Needed Me • and more.
00101936..$12.95

234. Disney Love Songs
15 songs, including: Beauty and the Beast • Can You Feel the Love Tonight • Candle on the Water • How Will I Know My Love? • So This Is Love • A Whole New World • and more.
00100042..$6.95

235. Elvis Presley Anthology
53 songs, including: All Shook Up • Are You Lonesome Tonight • Blue Suede Shoes • Can't Help Falling in Love • Don't Be Cruel (To a Heart That's True) • Heartbreak Hotel • Hound Dog • In the Ghetto • Love Me Tender • Return to Sender • Suspicious Minds • and more.
00101581..$14.95

237. Rock Revival
25 top hits from the early rock era, including: Chantilly Lace • Don't Be Cruel • Louie Louie • Splish Splash • The Twist • Wooly Bully • more.
00290056..$7.95

238. 25 Top Christmas Songs
25 of the best Christmas songs ever, together in one book. Songs include: Do You Hear What I Hear • Have Yourself a Merry Little Christmas • Silver Bells • Sleigh Ride • Santa Claus Is Coming to Town • Here Comes Santa Claus • Frosty the Snow Man • and more.
00290059..$7.95

239. Big Book of Children's Songs
Over 80 songs, including: Be Kind to Your Web-Footed Friends • Bingo • Goober Peas • He's Got the Whole World in His Hands • John Jacob Jingleheimer Schmidt • Kumbaya • Sailing Sailing • Twinkle, Twinkle Little Star • and more.
00290170..$12.95

240. Home for the Holidays
23 favorites, including: (There's No Place Like) Home for the Holidays • I'll Be Home for Christmas • The Little Drummer Boy • Rockin' Around the Christmas Tree • We Wish You a Merry Christmas • and more.
00001314..$6.95

241. Christmas Around the World
24 international carols: Angels We Have Heard on High • Deck the Hall • Fum, Fum, Fum • The Holly and the Ivy • Jingle Bells • O Little Town of Bethlehem • The Sleep of the Infant Jesus • Silent Night • and more.
00100061..$5.95

242. Les Misérables
13 songs from the musical sensation. Includes: Castle on a Cloud • I Dreamed a Dream • On My Own • and many more.
00290209..$10.95

244. Songs of the '80s
43 big hits from the 80's, featuring: Careless Whisper • Ebony and Ivory • Endless Love • Every Breath You Take • Hard Habit to Break • I Want to Know What Love Is • Kokomo • Lost in Your Eyes • I'll Be Loving You (Forever) • We Didn't Start the Fire • Sailing • These Dreams • Total Eclipse of the Heart • What's Love Got to Do With It • With or Without You.
00290242..$14.95

245. The Best of Simon & Garfunkel
19 songs, including: Bridge over Troubled Water • Fifty Ways to Leave Your Lover • Mrs. Robinson • Scarborough Fair • The Sound of Silence • Still Crazy After All These Years • and more.
00100041..$8.95

246. A Treasury of Songs
An outstanding collection of 76 contemporary favorites, including: What the World Needs Now Is Love • To All the Girls I've Loved Before • Raindrops Keep Falling on My Head • Sailing • Just the Way You Are • American Pie • I Write the Songs • Piano Man • and many more.
00102081..$17.95

247. Top Country Favorites
19 of country's best, including: All The Gold In California • Forever And Ever, Amen • God Bless The U.S.A. • Help Me Make It Through The Night • Kiss You All Over • Thank God And Greyhound.
00290264..$6.95

248. Disney's The Little Mermaid
The matching folio to this hit Disney movie. Eight songs, including the Oscar-winning "Under The Sea." Also: Part of Your World • Kiss the Girl • Fathoms Below • more.
00102108..$12.95

250. Classic TV Tunes
33 favorites, including: The Addams Family Theme • Bandstand Boogie • Bonanza • The Brady Bunch • Where Everybody Knows Your Name • I Love Lucy • Mission: Impossible Theme • The Odd Couple • Theme from "Route 66" • and more.
00100048..$9.95

251. The Phantom of the Opera
Nine songs from this Broadway smash, including: All I Ask Of You • The Point Of No Return • The Phantom Of The Opera • and more.
00102113..$14.95

252. Andy Griffith – I Love to Tell the Story
25 timeless hymns from the popular recording, including: Amazing Grace • How Great Thou Art • The Old Rugged Cross/Near the Cross • Sweet Hour of Prayer/What a Friend We Have in Jesus • We're Marching to Zion/When the Saints Go Marching In • and more.
00100065..$7.95

253. The Best Movie Songs Ever
A grand collection of 67 songs, including: Alfie • Beauty and the Beast • Born Free • Endless Love • Theme from "Jurassic Park" • Moon River • Que Sera, Sera • Somewhere Out There • Tears in Heaven • Unchained Melody • The Way We Were • and more.
00100064..$14.95

255. The Adult Contemporary Songbook
49 of today's best light hits, including: And So It Goes • Black Velvet • Fields of Gold • How Can We Be Lovers • I Will Always Love You • Sacrifice • Somewhere Out There • You Give Good Love • more.
00102311..$15.95

256. Broadway Waltzes
39 favorites in 3/4 time, from shows like: Can-Can • Kiss Me, Kate • Phantom of the Opera • South Pacific • more. Songs include Allez-Vous-En, Go Away • Do I Hear a Waltz? • Edelweiss • Try to Remember • more.
00102319..$9.95

257. Broadway Love Songs
49 romantic favorites from top Broadway shows. Songs include: All I Ask of You • Bewitched • I've Grown Accustomed to Her Face • Love Changes Everything • So in Love • Unexpected Song • We Kiss in a Shadow • and more.
00102320..$10.95

258. Broadway Ballads
Over 30 sentimental favorites from classic shows and contemporary blockbusters. Songs include: All I Ask of You • Bewitched • I Dreamed a Dream • Memory • My Funny Valentine • On My Own • People • Send in the Clowns • September Song • Smoke Gets in Your Eyes • Sun and Moon • Unexpected Song • What I Did for Love • and many more.
00102321..$9.95

260. Mister Rogers' Songbook
This terrific collection includes 25 songs from the "You're Growing" and "Bedtime" recordings, including: Are You Brave? • It's Such a Good Feeling • Please Don't Think It's Funny • Won't You Be My Neighbor • and more.
00102322..$8.95

261. The Best of Andrew Lloyd Webber
15 of his very best, including: All I Ask of You • Don't Cry for Me Argentina • I Don't Know How to Love Him • Memory • The Music of the Night • and more.
00102306 ....$12.95

262. Elvis Presley – His Love Songs
21 favorites, including: Ain't That Loving You Baby • Can't Help Falling in Love • I Want You, I Need You, I Love You • It's Now or Never • Love Me Tender • (Let Me Be Your) Teddy Bear • and more.
00100067 ....$7.95

263. Songs of the 1890s
Over 50 favorites from the Gay '90s, featuring: America, the Beautiful • The Band Played On • Hello! Ma Baby • Maple Leaf Rag • My Wild Irish Rose • O Sole Mio • The Sidewalks of New York • Stars and Stripes Forever • more.
00102299 ....$10.95

264. Songs of the 1900s (1900 - 1909)
Over 50 top turn-of-the-century tunes, including: Anchors Aweigh • Bill Bailey • By the Light of the Silvery Moon • Give My Regards to Broadway • Mary's a Grand Old Name • Meet Me in St. Louis • Shine on Harvest Moon • Sweet Adeline • Take Me Out to the Ball Game • Waltzing Matilda • The Yankee Doodle Boy • You're a Grand Old Flag • and more.
00102300 ....$10.95

265. Songs of the 1910s
Over 50 of the best songs from the teens, including: After You've Gone • Alexander's Ragtime Band • Danny Boy • Let Me Call You Sweetheart • My Melancholy Baby • 'Neath the Southern Moon • Peg O' My Heart • Rock-A-Bye Your Baby With a Dixie Melody • When Irish Eyes Are Smiling • You Made Me Love You • and more.
00102301 ....$10.95

266. Latin Hits
21 spicey songs, including: Adios • Always in My Heart • Blame It on the Bossa Nova • Brazil • Don't Cry for Me Argentina • How Insensitive • More • One Note Samba • Perhaps, Perhaps, Perhaps • Summer Samba • and more.
00100063 ....$6.95

267. Songs of Inspiration
26 spiritual songs, including: Abide With Me • Battle Hymn of the Republic • Jesus Loves Me • Ode to Joy • and more.
00001265 ....$5.95

268. The Branson Songbook
19 songs played on the stages of America's new music mecca. Features: Blue Velvet • Gentle on My Mind • The Branson Shuffle • Through the Years • Tulsa Time • and more.
00100002 ....$8.95

269. Love That Latin Beat
20 songs, including: Amapola • Besame Mucho • The Breeze and I • The Girl from Ipanema • Granada • The Look of Love • Mambo Jambo • Meditation • Never on Sunday • Perfidia • Quiet Nights of Quiet Stars • What a Diff'rence a Day Made • and more.
00100062 ....$7.95

270. New Age Melodies
20 beautiful melodies composed by Laurens Van Rooyen. Includes: Imaginary Landscapes • Just a Simple Love Song • Mother and Son • Reflections • and more.
00102289 ....$8.95

271. The Best of Mary Chapin Carpenter
16 great songs by Mary Chapin Carpenter, including: Come On Come On • Down at the Twist and Shout • I Feel Lucky • I Take My Chances • He Thinks He'll Keep Her • and more.
00102333 ....$7.95

272. The Best of Kenny G
16 of Kenny G's greatest, including: Forever in Love • Going Home • Joy of Life • Sade • Silhouette • Songbird • and more.
00102291 ....$7.95

73. Country Women of the '90s
27 hits by stars like: Mary Chapin Carpenter, Reba McEntire, Faith Hill, Trisha Yearwood, Kathy Mattea, Tanya Tucker, and more. Songs include: Down at the Twist and Shout • I Feel Lucky • No One Else on Earth • She Is His Only Need • Take It Like a Man • Wild One • more.
00102309 ....$10.95

275. Classical Hits – Bach, Beethoven & Brahms
Features 31 themes from favorite compositions, including: Arioso • Sheep May Safely Graze • The Moonlight Sonata • Hungarian Dance No. 5.
00102248 ....$6.95

276. Classical Hits – Operetta Magic
24 themes from favorite operettas, including: Naughty Marietta • Die Fledermaus • The Merry Widow • Babes in Toyland • The Pirates of Penzance • and more.
00102249 ....$6.95

277. Classical Hits – Italian Masters
28 favorite themes, including works by Monteverdi, Paganini, Puccini, Rossini, Verdi, Vivaldi, and more.
00102250 ....$6.95

278. Classical Hits – A Night at the Ballet
32 famous dances, including selections from Swan Lake, The Nutcracker, and more.
00102251 ....$6.95

279. Classical Hits – A Night at the Opera
Over 20 favorite songs from operas such as Carmen, Romeo and Juliet, The Marriage of Figaro, La Boheme, Faust, and more.
00102252 ....$6.95

280. Classical Hits – A Night at the Symphony
29 themes from symphonic masterpieces, including: Also Sprach Zarathustra • Eine Kleine Nachtmusik • The Unfinished Symphony • The William Tell Overture • and more.
00102253 ....$6.95

282. Pooh
Songs from Classic Winnie the Pooh Features
10 songs from everyone's favorite bear, including: Heffalumps and Woozles • A Rather Blustery Day • Rumbly in My Tumbly • Winnie the Pooh • The Wonderful Thing About Tiggers • and more.
00100066 ....$6.95

283. The Best Jazz Standards Ever
73 of the best, including: All of You • April in Paris • Autumn in New York • Bewitched • Body and Soul • Don't Get Around Much Anymore • Isn't It Romantic? • Misty • Mona Lisa • Satin Doll • Tangerine • When I Fall in Love • and more.
00100068 ....$12.95

284. Contemporary Movie Favorites
Over 25 songs, including: The Addams Family • Beauty and the Beast • (Everything I Do) I Do It for You • It Had to Be You • Kokomo • The Shoop Shoop Song (It's in His Kiss) • Somewhere Out There • Unchained Melody • and more.
00102260 ....$8.95

286. Early Rock and Roll
24 classics, including: All Shook Up • At the Hop • Do Wah Diddy Diddy • Duke of Earl • The Great Pretender • Rock Around the Clock • Wake Up Little Susie • and more.
00100071 ....$6.95

287. A Year in Song
A song for every season! 50 in all, including: America the Beautiful • April Showers • Auld Lang Syne • Easter Parade • Graduation Day • Happy Hanukkah, My Friend • Indian Summer • The Lusty Month of May • M-O-T-H-E-R • My Funny Valentine • Silver Bells • Taxman • When Irish Eyes Are Smiling • and more.
00100070 ....$12.95

288. Sing-A-Long Christmas Favorites
18 seasonal sing-a-longs: Blue Christmas • Deck the Halls • Frosty the Snowman • Jingle Bells • O Christmas Tree • Silver Bells • more. Features 12 pull-out sets of lyrics for each song.
00100022 ....$6.95

289. Sing-A-Long Christmas Carols
18 holiday songs: Away in a Manger • The First Noel • Joy to the World • O Holy Night • Silent Night • What Child Is This • more. Features 12 pull-out sets of lyrics for each song.
00100023 ....$6.95

290. "My Heart Will Go On" and 15 Other Top Movie Hits
16 favorites from films, including: Chariots of Fire • Colors of the Wind • Forrest Gump – Main Title • I Finally Found Someone • I Say a Little Prayer • Misson: Impossible Theme • You Must Love Me • and more.
00100073 ....$7.95

291. Children's Christmas Songs
30 holiday favorites, including: Frosty the Snow Man • Jingle Bells • Jolly Old St. Nicholas • Rudolph, the Red-Nosed Reindeer • Up on the Housetop • and more!
00102230...$7.95

292. Really Big Book of Children's Songs
A classic collection of over 60 songs, including: Any Dream Will Do • Dance Little Bird (The Chicken Dance) • Hakuna Matata • I Won't Grow Up • Kum Ba Yah • Sesame Street Theme • So Long, Farewell • Winnie the Pooh • Won't You Be My Neighbor? • and more.
00100072...$12.95

293. Movie Classics – 2nd Edition
35 songs, including: An Affair to Remember • Buttons and Bows • Theme from Ice Castles • Love Is a Many-Splendored Thing • Moon River • New York, New York • Over the Rainbow • The Shadow of Your Smile • Talk to the Animals • A Time for Us • The Way We Were • and more.
00102124...$8.95

294. Old-Fashioned Love Songs
Features 50 heart-warming favorites, including: Always • Danke Schoen • For Me and My Gal • Have You Ever Been Lonely? • Heart and Soul • I Can't Give You Anything but Love • Let Me Call You Sweetheart • Somewhere, My Love • You Made Me Love You • more.
00100069...$9.95

295. More Songs of the 90's
Easy arrangements of over 30 contemporary hits: All by Myself • Blue • Building a Mystery • Butterfly Kisses • Change the World • Don't Speak • Give Me One Reason • I Don't Want to Wait • The Lord of the Dance • My Heart Will Go On • You Were Meant for Me • more.
00100074...$12.95

296. Best of Cole Porter
Features 23 timeless treasures: Anything Goes • Begin the Beguine • Don't Fence Me In • From This Moment On • I Get a Kick out of You • I Love Paris • I Love You • I've Got You Under My Skin • In the Still of the Night • It's De-Lovely • Just One of Those Things • Love for Sale • Night and Day • You Do Something to Me • You'd Be So Nice to Come Home To • You're the Top • more.
00100075...$6.95

297. Best TV Themes
21 TV classics, including: Theme from "Cheers" • Entertainment Tonight • The Hill Street Blues Theme • Jeopardy Theme • Newhart • St. Elsewhere • Thank You for Being A Friend • and more!
00102126...$6.95

298. Beautiful Love Songs
26 sentimental favorites, featuring: For Once in My Life • The Greatest Gift of All • I Honestly Love You • I Just Called to Say I Love You • Love Story • Up Where We Belong • You Are So Beautiful • You Light Up My Life.
00102130...$7.95

299. The Vaudeville Songbook
The story, stars and 25 songs of Vaudeville, including: After You've Gone • April Showers • Bill Bailey, Won't You Please Come Home • Chinatown, My Chinatown • The Darktown Strutters' Ball • A Second Hand Rose • Swanee • more.
00100077...$6.95

300. Light Classics
More than 20 terrific waltzes, marches, operetta favorites and Italian songs, including: By the Beautiful Blue Danube • Can Can • Carnival of Venice • 'O Sole Mio • Santa Lucia • Semper Fidelis • Stars and Stripes Forever • more!
00100079...$6.95

301. Kidsongs
Contains over 40 favorite children's songs, with color-coded music that corresponds to the enclosed color-coded key stickers, so it's easy to play! Also includes musical puzzles, pictures to color, fun things to learn, and these great songs: Are You Sleeping? • Beautiful Brown Eyes • Can-Can • Jack Sprat • Oh, Susanna • This Old Man • and many more.
00001102...$9.95

302. The Travis Tritt Songbook
18 songs, including: Drift Off To Dream • Help Me Hold On • Here's a Quarter (Call Someone Who Cares) • Put Some Drive in Your Country • and more.
00102222...$8.95

304. Hollywood Love Songs
Features 9 hot big screen favorites: Always in My Heart (Siempre En Mi Corazón) • Can't Help Falling in Love • I Finally Found Someone • Love Me Tender • Moon River • My Heart Will Go On • Somewhere, My Love • True Love • When I Fall in Love.
00100078...$8.95

306. The Irving Berlin Collection
A massive collection of 75 Berlin classics to treasure. Includes: Alexander's Ragtime Band • Always • Be Careful, It's My Heart • Blue Skies • Easter Parade • God Bless America • Heat Wave • Puttin' on the Ritz • There's No Business Like Show Business • White Christmas • and many more!
00102147...$14.95

308. The Greatest American Songbook
A 37-song salute to American heart-warmers such as: America, the Beautiful • The Eagle • From a Distance • God Bless The U.S.A. • Imagine • The Star Spangled Banner • Stars and Stripes Forever • Yankee Doodle Boy • and more.
00102182...$8.95

310. Scott Joplin's Greatest Hits
15 of the best from the King of Ragtime, including: The Entertainer • Maple Leaf Rag • Bethena • The Easy Winners • and more.
00001545...$5.95

311. The Platters Anthology
19 songs from this classic R&B group and an 11-page introduction with lots of photos! Songs include: (You've Got) The Magic Touch • Only You (And You Alone) • The Great Pretender • My Prayer • Twilight Time • Smoke Gets in Your Eyes • and many more.
00001580...$7.95

312. Jump, Jive, Wail & Swing
42 big swinging hits arranged in our famous E-Z Play Today notation. Includes: Bandstand Boogie • Christopher Columbus • In the Mood • It Don't Mean a Thing (If It Ain't Got That Swing) • Java Jive • Jump, Jive an' Wail • Lazy River • Marie • Opus One • Steppin' Out with My Baby • Take the "A" Train • more.
00100083...$10.95

313. Carly Simon – Greatest Hits
A compilation of 13 of her best, including: Anticipation • Haven't Got Time for the Pain • Jesse • Mockingbird • Nobody Does It Better • You're So Vain • and more.
00102190...$7.95

314. Miss Saigon
Eleven songs from the Broadway spectacular, including: The American Dream • The Heat Is On in Saigon • Sun and Moon • I'd Give My Life for You • The Last Night of the World • and more.
00102191...$10.95

315. Broadway Musicals Show by Show – 1891-1916
33 classics with background text from shows such as: Robin Hood, Florodora, Babes In Toyland, The Merry Widow, and more. Songs include: After the Ball • The Bowery • Give My Regards to Broadway • Kiss Me Again • March of the Toys • Mary's a Grand Old Name • My Hero • Simple Melody • Streets of New York • more.
00102197...$8.95

316. Broadway Musicals Show by Show – 1917-1929
41 songs and interesting trivia from the era's most popular shows. Songs include: Can't Help Lovin' Dat Man • Fascinating Rhythm • How Long Has This Been Going On? • Ol' Man River • A Pretty Girl Is Like a Melody • Tea for Two • You Do Something to Me • and more.
00102196...$9.95

317. Broadway Musicals Show by Show – 1930-1939
A collection of 46 songs and notes from the decade's biggest Broadway hits, including: Anything Goes, Porgy And Bess, On Your Toes and more. Songs include: Begin the Beguine • Falling in Love with Love • I Get a Kick Out of You • My Funny Valentine • Smoke Gets in Your Eyes • Strike Up the Band • and more.
00102195...$9.95

318. Broadway Musicals Show by Show – 1940-1949
Show descriptions by renowned Broadway historian Stanley Green, and 48 songs: Another Op'nin, Another Show • Bali Ha'i • Bewitched • If I Loved You • New York, New York • Some Enchanted Evening • The Surrey with the Fringe on Top • You'll Never Walk Alone • more.
00102194...$10.95

319. Broadway Musicals Show by Show – 1950-1959
49 songs from classics such as: My Fair Lady, West Side Story, The Sound Of Music, and more. Songs include: Edelweiss • Getting to Know You • I Could Have Danced All Night • Let Me Entertain You • Mack the Knife • Maria • Shall We Dance? • Somewhere • and more.
00102192...$10.95

320. Broadway Musicals Show by Show – 1960-1971
43 songs and background text from shows such as Oliver!, Cabaret, Camelot, Hello, Dolly!, Fiddler On The Roof, Jesus Christ Superstar, Mame, and more. Songs include: As Long As He Needs Me • Consider Yourself • Day by Day • I Don't Know How to Love Him • People • Sunrise, Sunset • Try to Remember • We Need a Little Christmas •and more.
00102193..$12.95

321. Broadway Musicals Show by Show – 1972-1988
30 songs from this era of big productions like Phantom Of The Opera, Evita, La Cage Aux Folles, Les Miserables, A Chorus Line, Cats, and more. Songs include: All I Ask of You • I Am What I Am • I Dreamed a Dream • Memory • The Music of the Night • On My Own • What I Did for Love • and more.
00102198..$12.95

322. Dixieland
23 Dixie delights, including: After You've Gone • Basin Street Blues • Do You Know What It Means to Miss New Orleans? • King Porter Stomp • Maple Leaf Rag • Mississippi Mud • Some of These Days • Sugar Blues • more.
00100080..$6.95

323. The Best of Rod Stewart
30 Stewart classics, including: Downtown Train • The First Cut Is the Deepest • Forever Young • Infatuation • Maggie May • Passion • Rhythm of My Heart • This Old Heart of Mine • Tonight's the Night • You're in My Heart • Young Turks • and more.
00102200..$10.95

324. Gone Country! – Hits of the '90s
20 big hits that are easy to play, including: Ain't That Lonely Yet • Bobbie Ann Mason • Chattahoochee • Gone Country • The Heart Is a Lonely Hunter • Mi Vida Loca (My Crazy Life) • She's Not the Cheatin' Kind • XXX's and OOO's (An American Girl) • You Ain't Much Fun • and more.
00100026..$9.95

326. Swinging Love Songs
35 favorite love songs of the swing era: Aquellos Ojos Verdes (Green Eyes) • Blue Skies • Body and Soul • Cheek to Cheek • Lazy River • L-O-V-E • Makin' Whoopee! • My Romance • Side by Side • The Way You Look Tonight • more.
00100081..$9.95

327. Tonight at the Lounge
26 songs of the lounge circuit: Cabaret • Cry Me a River • Downtown • Georgia on My Mind • I Will Survive • Lazy River • My Funny Valentine • Spanish Eyes • Stayin' Alive • That Old Black Magic • That's Amore • You've Lost That Lovin' Feelin' • more.
00100082..$7.95

328. Beauty And The Beast
8 songs including: Be Our Guest • Beauty and the Beast • Belle • Gaston • Something There • and more.
00102201..$9.95

330. The Nutcracker Suite
Eight pieces from this famous suite, including: Dance of the Sugar Plum Fairy • Dance of the Reed Flutes • Waltz of the Flowers • and more.
00102275..$5.95

332. The Rolling Stones Greatest Hits
13 classics, including: Angie • Beast of Burden • Hang Fire • It's Only Rock 'N' Roll • Miss You • Start Me Up • Waiting on a Friend • and more.
00102204..$7.95

333. Great Gospel Favorites
19 songs of faith, including: Amazing Grace • Give Me That Old Time Religion • His Eye Is on the Sparrow • Just a Closer Walk with Thee • The Old Rugged Cross • Precious Memories • There Is Power in the Blood • and more
00100092..$6.95

334. American Spirituals
22 traditional favorites, including: Every Time I Feel the Spirit • Nobody Knows the Trouble I've Seen • Rock-a-My Soul • Swing Low, Sweet Chariot • Wayfaring Stranger • more.
00100091..$6.95

335. Steven Curtis Chapman
Easy arrangements of 14 of his hits, including: For the Sake of the Call • The Great Adventure • His Eyes • More to This Life • Signs of Life • Treasure Island • Weak Days • When You Are a Soldier • more.
00100085..$10.95

337. Classical Themes from the Movies
Over 25 well-known pieces from movies like 2001: A Space Odyssey, Ordinary People, Pretty Woman, Moonstruck, Fatal Attraction, Amadeus, and more! Selections include: Also Sprach Zarathustra • Ave Maria • Blue Danube Waltz • The Minute Waltz • Toreador Song from Carmen • and more.
00102205..$6.95

338. Complete Star Trek® Theme Music
Includes 13 themes from the Star Trek movies and TV series, including: Star Trek® Insurrection • Theme from Star Trek® • Star Trek: Deep Space Nine® • Star Trek®: First Contact • Star Trek®: The Motion Picture • Star Trek® III: The Search for Spock • Star Trek® II: The Wrath of Khan • and more.
00100086..$9.95

339. Grease Is Still the Word
23 songs from the hit movie Grease, now celebrating its 20th anniversary. Includes: Beauty School Dropout • Born to Hand Jive • Love Is a Many-Splendored Thing • Sandy • Summer Nights • We Go Together • more.
00100084..$10.95

340. Billboard Top Country Songs of the '60s
A great compilation of 62 songs and background text on this era of country music. Includes: Act Naturally • Crazy • D-I-V-O-R-C-E • Daddy Sang Bass • Green Green Grass of Home • King of the Road • Make the World Go Away • Okie from Muskogee • Ruby, Don't Take Your Love to Town • She's Got You • and more.
00102225..$14.95

341. Billboard Top Country Songs of the '70s
62 songs complete with text on this era in country music. Songs include: Come On In • Daydreams About Night Things • Every Which Way But Loose • The Gambler • Help Me Make It Through the Night • (Hey Won't You Play) Another Somebody Done Somebody Wrong Song • I'm Not Lisa • Luckenbach, Texas • Mammas Don't Let Your Babies Grow Up to Be Cowboys • and more.
00102226..$14.95

342. Billboard Top Country Songs of the '80s
An historical overview and 53 songs and text from the decade's biggest country stars. Includes: Coward of the County • Forever and Ever, Amen • God Bless the U.S.A. • Grandpa (Tell Me 'Bout the Good Old Days) • I Was Country When Country Wasn't Cool • I Wouldn't Have Missed It for the World • Islands in the Stream • and more.
00102227..$14.95

344. Billboard Top Rock 'N' Roll Hits of the '70s
50 of the decade's biggest hits, including: All Right Now • Band on the Run • Bennie and the Jets • Crocodile Rock • Free Bird • I Will Survive • I'm Just a Singer in a Rock 'N Roll Band • I've Got the Music in Me • Jesus Is Just All Right with Me • Knock Three Times • Maggie May • Me and Bobby McGee • Midnight Train to Georgia • My Sweet Lord • Night Fever • Philadelphia Freedom • Reelin' in the Years • She's Some Kind of Wonderful • Silly Love Song • Takin' Care of Business • We Just Disagree • and more.
00102246..$14.95

345. Billboard Top Rock 'N' Roll Hits of the '80s
Over 40 songs that topped the rock charts in the 80s, including: Addicted to Love • Every Breath You Take • Every Rose Has Its Thorn • Express Yourself • Faith • I Love Rock 'N' Roll • I Want to Know What Love Is • Livin' on a Prayer • Straight Up • Total Eclipse of the Heart • We Didn't Start the Fire • What's Love Got to Do With It • With or Without You • and more.
00102247..$14.95

346. Big Book of Christmas Songs
125 wonderful Christmas songs, including: All Through the Night • Christ Was Born on Christmas Day • The Coventry Carol • The First Noel • Good King Wenceslas • Here We Come A-Wassailing • It Came Upon the Midnight Clear • Noel! Noel! • O Christmas Tree • O Holy Night • Silent Night • The Twelve Days of Christmas • What Child Is This? • and more.
00102235..$14.95

348. Selections from Messiah
18 selections from George Frideric Handel's beloved Messiah, featuring the famous "Hallelujah."
00102239..$6.95

349. The Giant Book of American Folksongs
74 songs celebrating America's heritage: Buffalo Gals • The Cruel War Is Raging • Down in the Valley • Frankie and Johnny • I've Been Working on the Railroad • Simple Gifts • When Johnny Comes Marching Home • more.
00100089 E-Z Play Today #349 ....$9.95

350. Billboard Songbook Series – The Best of 1955-1959

This compilation features five books under one cover–80 songs in all, with extensive notes on the era and its hits! Song highlights include: Earth Angel • Unchained Melody • Blue Suede Shoes • Hound Dog • All Shook Up • Blueberry Hill • Peggy Sue • At the Hop • Great Balls of Fire • Sixteen Candles • Smoke Gets in Your Eyes • and more.
00102140 .... $19.95

354. Mighty Big Book of Children's Songs

Includes 60 kids' classics: Do Your Ears Hang Low? • The Grouch Song • Hakuna Matata • Hush, Little Baby • Little White Duck • Sesame Street Theme • Winnie the Pooh • You've Got a Friend in Me • more.
00100087 .... $12.95

355. Smoky Mountain Gospel Favorites

A collection of 36 treasured hymns: Amazing Grace • At the Cross • I Am Bound for the Promised Land • I Love to Tell the Story • The Old Rugged Cross • Power in the Blood • Since Jesus Came into My Heart • What a Friend We Have in Jesus • When We All Get to Heaven • more.
00100088 .... $8.95

356. John Tesh

15 of John Tesh's best songs including: April Song • Barcelona • Bastille Day • Give Me Forever (I Do) • Goodnight Moon • Grand Passion • The Homecoming • In a Child's Eyes • Venezia • Wishing for Home • more.
02500128 .... $8.95

357. Disney's Tarzan

8 songs from Disney's *Tarzan*, including: Son of Man • Strangers like Me • Trashin' the Camp • Two Worlds • Two Worlds (Finale) • Two Worlds (Reprise) • You'll Be in My Heart • You'll Be in My Heart (Pop Version).
00100094 .... $9.95

358. Gospel Songs of Hank Williams

20 soul-stirring favorites from the legendary Hank Williams: Are You Walkin' and A-Talkin' for the Lord • Dear Brother • A Home in Heaven • House of Gold • How Can You Refuse Him Now • I Saw the Light • Jesus Is Calling • Wealth Won't Save Your Soul • When God Comes and Gathers His Jewels • more.
00100093 .... $7.95

359. 100 Years of Song

This unique collection contains 100 songs, one for each year of the 20th century. Includes: Alexander's Ragtime Band • Bewitched • All I Ask of You • All You Need Is Love • From a Distance • Heart and Soul • My Heart Will Go On • Rock Around the Clock • Star Dust • A String of Pearls • The Way We Were • and more.
00100095 .... $17.95

360. More 100 Years of Song

This follow-up edition contains a completely different selection of songs from each year the century. Includes: Give My Regards to Broadway • Manhattan • The Way You Look Tonight • Route 66 • Mona Lisa • All Shook Up • Hey Jude • Chariots of Fire • Can You Feel the Love Tonight • more.
00100096 .... $17.95

361. Around the Christmas Tree

Features 27 traditional carols including: Angels from the Realms of Glory • Coventry Carol • Go Tell It on the Mountain • In the Bleak Midwinter • O Christmas Tree • Silent Night • Sussex Carol • Wassail, Wassail • We Wish You a Merry Christmas • more.
00100098 .... $6.95

362. Disney's Aladdin

The matching folio to the Disney blockbuster. Six songs, including: One Jump Ahead • Prince Ali • Friend Like Me • A Whole New World • and more.
00102266 .... $9.95

363. It's the Holiday Season

Simple arrangements of 20 songs of the season: Blue Christmas • Do You Hear What I Hear • Grandma Got Run Over by a Reindeer • Happy Holiday • A Holly Jolly Christmas • Wonderful Christmastime • more.
00100097 .... $7.95

364. Love Ballads

Cherry Lane Music
18 great ballads: Always • Annie's Song • Butterfly Kisses • For All We Know • Hard Habit to Break • Leaving on a Jet Plane • Please Come to Boston • Somewhere Out There • You Must Love Me • Your Song • more.
02500152 .... $7.95

365. Top Country Hits

Cherry Lane Music
Simple arrangements of 17 super hits: Achy Breaky Heart • Ain't That Lonely Yet • Back Home Again • Gone Country • My Maria • She Is His Only Need • You Ain't Much Fun • more.
02500154 .... $7.95

366. Pop/Rock Hits

Cherry Lane Music
18 songs by top artists such as Celine Dion, Elton John, John Denver, Bon Jovi and more. Includes: All by Myself • Annie's Song • Blue Velvet • From a Distance • It's All Coming Back to Me Now • Rocket Man • more.
02500153 .... $7.95

367. More Songs of the '20s

Over 50 songs, including: Ain't We Got Fun? • All by Myself • Bill • Carolina in the Morning • Fascinating Rhythm • The Hawaiian Wedding Song • I Want to Be Bad • I'm Just Wild About Harry • Malagueña • Nobody Knows You When You're Down and Out • Someone to Watch Over Me • Yes, Sir, That's My Baby • and more.
00102292 .... $12.95

368. More Songs of the '30s

Over 50 songs, including: All The Things You Are • Begin the Beguine • A Fine Romance • I Only Have Eyes for You • In a Sentimental Mood • Just a Gigolo • Let's Call the Whole Thing Off • The Most Beautiful Girl in the World • Mad Dogs and Englishmen • Stompin' at the Savoy • Stormy Weather • Thanks for the Memory • The Very Thought of You • and more.
00102293 .... $12.95

369. More Songs of the '40s

Over 60 songs, including: Bali Ha'i • Be Careful, It's My Heart • A Dream Is a Wish Your Heart Makes • Five Guys Named Moe • Is You Is, or Is You Ain't (Ma' Baby) • The Last Time I Saw Paris • Old Devil Moon • San Antonio Rose • Some Enchanted Evening • Steppin' Out with My Baby • Take the "A" Train • Too Darn Hot • Zip-A-Dee-Doo-Dah • and more.
00102294 .... $12.95

370. More Songs of the '50s

Over 50 songs, including: All of You • Blueberry Hill • Chanson D'Amour • Charlie Brown • Do-Re-Mi • Hey, Good Lookin' • Hound Dog • I Could Have Danced All Night • Love and Marriage • Mack the Knife • Mona Lisa • My Favorite Things • Sixteen Tons • (Let Me Be Your) Teddy Bear • That's Amore • Yakety Yak • and more.
00102295 .... $12.95

371. More Songs of the '60s

Over 60 songs, including: Alfie • Baby Elephant Walk • Bonanza • Born to Be Wild • Eleanor Rigby • The Impossible Dream • Leaving on a Jet Plane • Moon River • Raindrops Keep Fallin' on My Head • Ruby, Don't Take Your Love to Town • Seasons in the Sun • Sweet Caroline • Tell Laura I Love Her • A Time for Us • What the World Needs Now • Wooly Bully • and more.
00102296 .... $12.95

372. More Songs of the '70s

Over 50 songs, including: Afternoon Delight • All by Myself • American Pie • Billy, Don't Be a Hero • The Candy Man • Happy Days • I Shot the Sheriff • Long Cool Woman (In a Black Dress) • Maggie May • On Broadway • She Believes in Me • She's Always a Woman • Spiders and Snakes • Star Wars • Taxi • You've Got a Friend • and more.
00102297 .... $12.95

373. More Songs of the '80s

Over 50 songs, including: Addicted to Love • Almost Paradise • Axel F • Call Me • Don't Know Much • Even the Nights Are Better • Footloose • Girls Just Want to Have Fun • The Heat Is On • Karma Chameleon • Longer • Straight Up • Take My Breath Away • Tell Her About It • We're in This Love Together • and more.
00102298 .... $12.95

374. Brooks and Dunn – Brand New Man

Ten songs from this hit-packed album, including: Boot Scootin' Boogie • Brand New Man • Lost and Found • My Next Broken Heart • Neon Moon • and more!
00102281 .... $6.95

375. The Songs of Bacharach & David

20 classic tunes from the talented team of Bacharach & David: Alfie • I Say a Little Prayer • I'll Never Fall in Love Again • The Look of Love • Raindrops Keep Fallin' on My Head • This Guy's in Love with You • Walk on By • What the World Needs Now Is Love • Wives and Lovers • more.
00100103 .... $7.95

379. Barbra Streisand – Back to Broadway

Matching folio to the legendary singer's album of classic and contemporary Broadway hits, including: The Music of the Night • Luck Be a Lady • Some Enchanted Evening • I Have a Love/One Hand, One Heart • plus six more.
00102307 .... $7.95

381. Mariah Carey – Music Box
Ten of Mariah's biggest hits, including: Dreamlover • Hero • Anytime You Need a Friend •Music Box • and more.
00102305...$7.95

382. Disney's The Lion King
Five songs from the hit Disney release: Be Prepared • Can You Feel the Love Tonight • I Just Can't Wait to Be King • Circle of Life • Hakuna Matata.
00102328...$12.95

383. 14 Top Hits
Features: Dreamlover • Fields of Gold • I Don't Wanna Fight • I'd Do Anything for Love • Ordinary World • and more.
00102327...$6.95

386. Disney's Pocahontas
Ten songs from the Disney hit, including: Colors of the Wind • Just Around the Riverbend • Savages • Mine, Mine, Mine • and more. Includes beautiful full-color photos from the film.
00100020...$12.95

387. Still More Songs of the '30s
Over 50 more favorites from the 30s, including: Blue Hawaii • Body and Soul • Cheek to Cheek • Down in the Depths (On the Ninetieth Floor) • How Deep Is the Ocean • My Romance • You Oughta Be in Pictures • and more.
00100009...$12.95

388. Still More Songs of the '40s
Over 50 more 40s favorites, including: (There'll Be Bluebirds Over) The White Cliffs of Dover • Don't Get Around Much Anymore • It's Been a Long, Long Time • Sentimental Journey • Stella by Starlight • Tangerine • and more.
00100011...$12.95

389. Still More Songs of the '50s
Over 50 more 50s favorites: A Dream Is a Wish Your Heart Makes • Autumn Leaves • Chantilly Lace • It's So Easy • Mister Sandman • Peggy Sue • Stranger in Paradise • Unchained Melody • Venus • Witchcraft • and more.
00100012...$12.95

390. Still More Songs of the '60s
More than 55 60s hits, including: (I'm Not Your) Steppin' Stone • (You Make Me Feel Like) A Natural Woman • Blame It on the Bossa Nova • Bobby's Girl • Do You Believe in Magic • Duke of Earl • Hey Jude • Leader of the Pack • and more.
00100006...$12.95

391. Still More Songs of the '70s
Over 50 hits of the 70s, like: Ain't No Way to Treat a Lady • Angie • Band on the Run • Do You Know Where You're Going To? • Green-Eyed Lady • I'm Easy • If • Midnight Blue • and more.
00100005...$12.95

E-Z Play Today Bound Collection Christmas Library
A treasury of Christmas magic in a special bound collection of four E-Z Play Today songbooks: Christmas Songs, That Christmas Feeling, Holly Season, and Christmas Time. 84 songs in all!
00100627...$19.80

THE GRAND STAND
Portable Music and Bookstand
(U.S. Patent No. 4,709,895.)

So versatile and unique, THE GRAND STAND portable bookstand demonstrates a wide variety of uses at home, in the office, in libraries...anywhere!

Perfect for all musicians, or for use at home:
- in the kitchen – great for cookbooks
- with the home computer – provides a handy stand for manuals
- for students' homework or music practice
- for do-it-yourselfers – in any work area

Also ideal as a typing stand, for reading or writing in a hospital or at bedtime, as a lectern for speakers at business meetings, and for many other uses! Lightweight and portable, THE GRAND STAND bookstand folds flat for carrying and fits easily into a schoolbag or briefcase.

Constructed of sturdy fiberboard covered in attractive and easy-to-clean vinyl, THE GRAND STAND bookstand is packaged in a handy folding carton for convenient storage.

This unique product also features a handy page retainer that holds large books with stiff bindings open, without restricting the view of the page.

00183284 Black...$12.95

FOR ORGANS, PIANOS & ELECTRONIC KEYBOARDS

THE LOGICAL STEP FROM E-Z PLAY TODAY

Here's the most logical, practical, and exciting next step for those who have become avid fans of E-Z Play Today music. Solo Today, for beginning and intermediate players, is a double-staff series for anyone ready to learn bass clef in the easiest way possible. Solo Today provides you with a logical answer to your need for more advanced material that is still easy-to-read and easy-to-play.

FEATURES OF THIS SERIES INCLUDE

• Solo Today is not a gimmick system … everything used is geared for the player who ultimately wants to progress to conventional music reading.

• Full-size books – large 9" x 12" format features easy-to-read, easy-to-play music instruction. Two instruction books, Step By Step Books A & B, provide an introduction to the series and present the fundamentals of more advanced playing techniques.

• Lyrics … most arrangements include words and music.

• Each song is arranged in enlarged, easy-to-read double-staffed notation. All songs basically use one or two notes in the melody and one or two note harmonies for the left hand. All appropriate chord symbols are given.

• Most up-to-date registrations…a general Registration Guide for most organs is available – helps customers obtain the sounds they want most. Brand name registration guides are also available.

• Optional pedal patterns are included with each arrangement so organists can create interesting bass line harmonies.

• Playing tips – the songbook is prefaced with a "Playing Tips" section that details the new notation and provides registration suggestions.

STEP BY STEP BOOK A

As the introduction book to the Solo Today series, this is the perfect learning tool for the beginning bass clef player. It's also the ideal "step-up" for the E-Z Play Today player wishing to play two-staff treble and bass clef notation. Familiar songs are written in a unique form of treble and bass clef notation and are slightly enlarged for easy reading.
00106965 ....$5.95

STEP BY STEP BOOK B

A continuation of the instruction presented in book A, introducing many more new skills. Many song favorites, included.
00106966 ....$5.95

TOP REQUESTS

Features 20 top tunes: After You've Gone • Autumn Leaves • Dinah • A Good Man Is Hard to Find • Hello, Dolly! • It's So Nice to Have a Man Around the House • Mame • Put on a Happy Face • Sentimental Journey • S'posin' • Tenderly • You Call Everybody Darling • and more.
00107000 ....$6.95

E-Z PLAY TODAY KEY STICKERS

These self-adhesive key stickers are for use with all keyboards. They come in a 9" x 12" package, with a listing of E-Z play books. Makes learning to play easy!

00100016 ....$2.50

E-Z PLAY TODAY ORGAN KEYBOARD GUIDES

Sturdy cardboard guides to help you quickly and easily learn the keyboard!

00100519 ....$2.50

90500035
1099

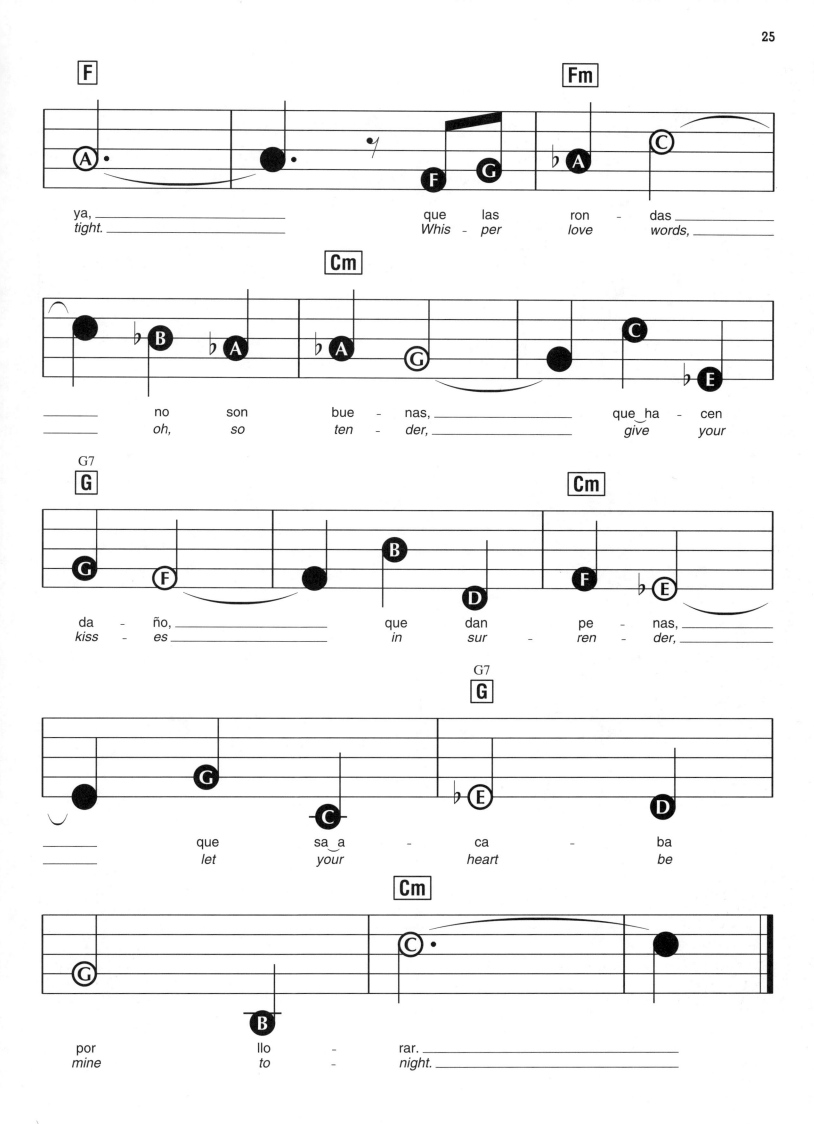

Perfidia

Registration 3
Rhythm: Rhumba or Latin

Words and Music by
Alberto Dominguez

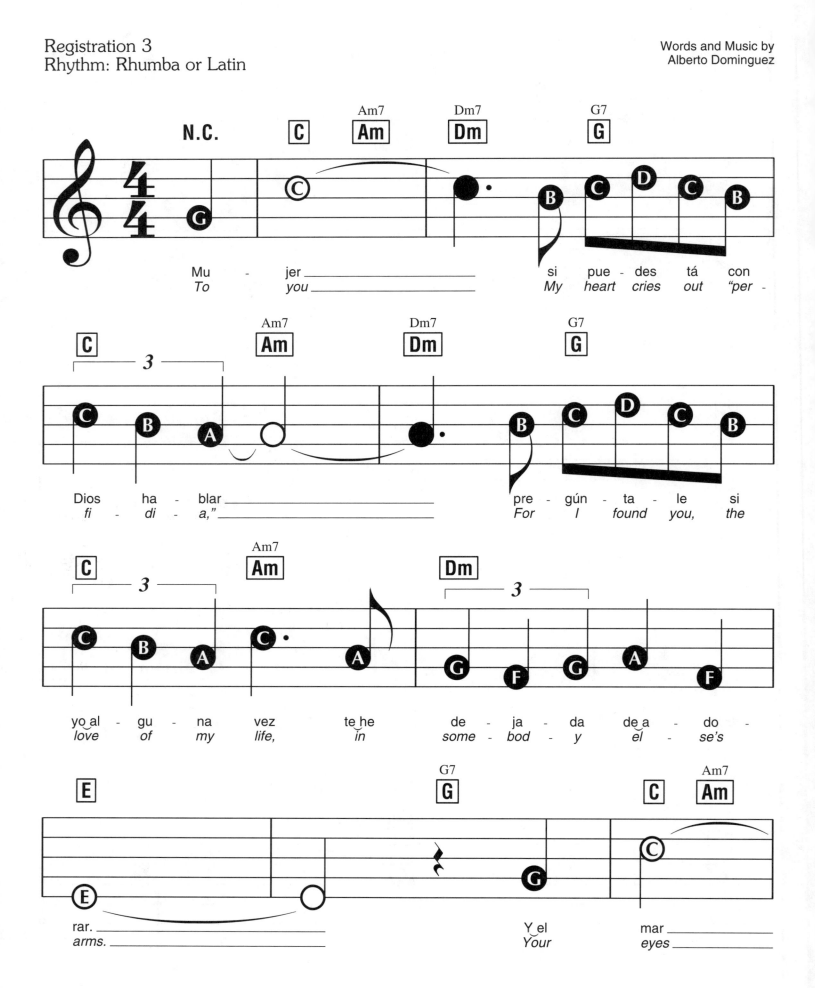

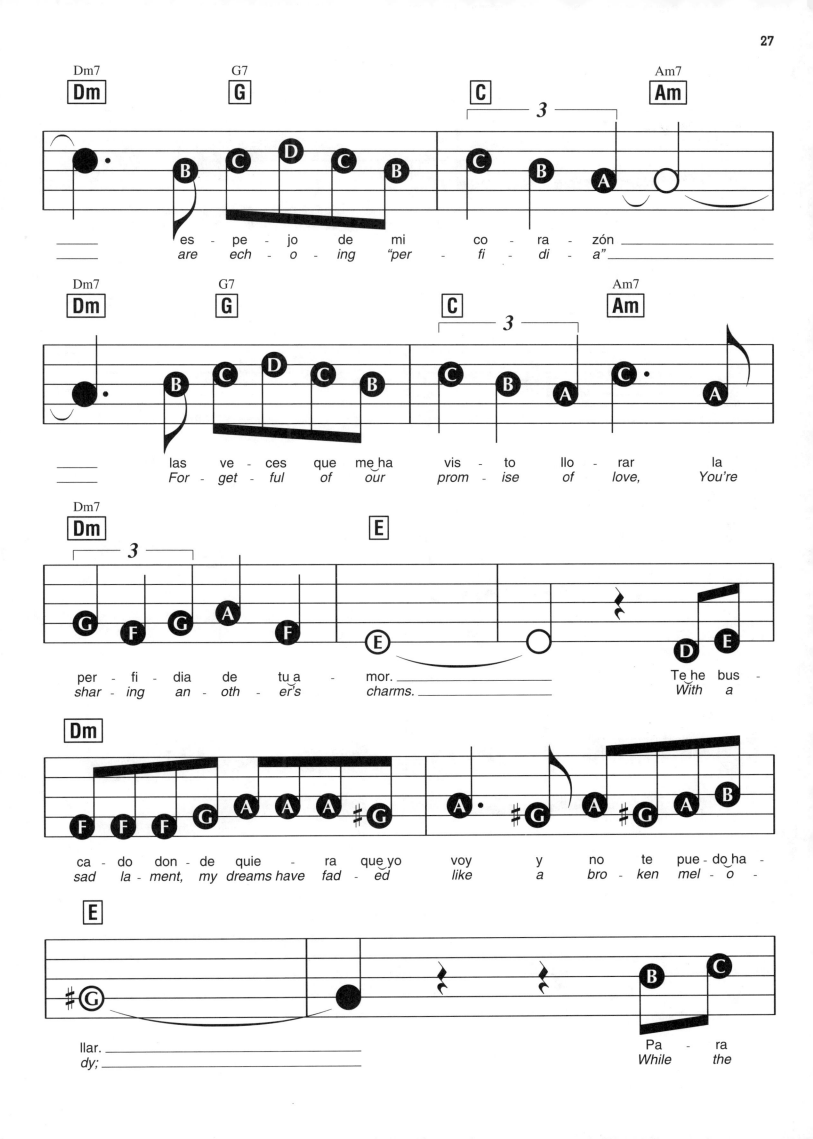

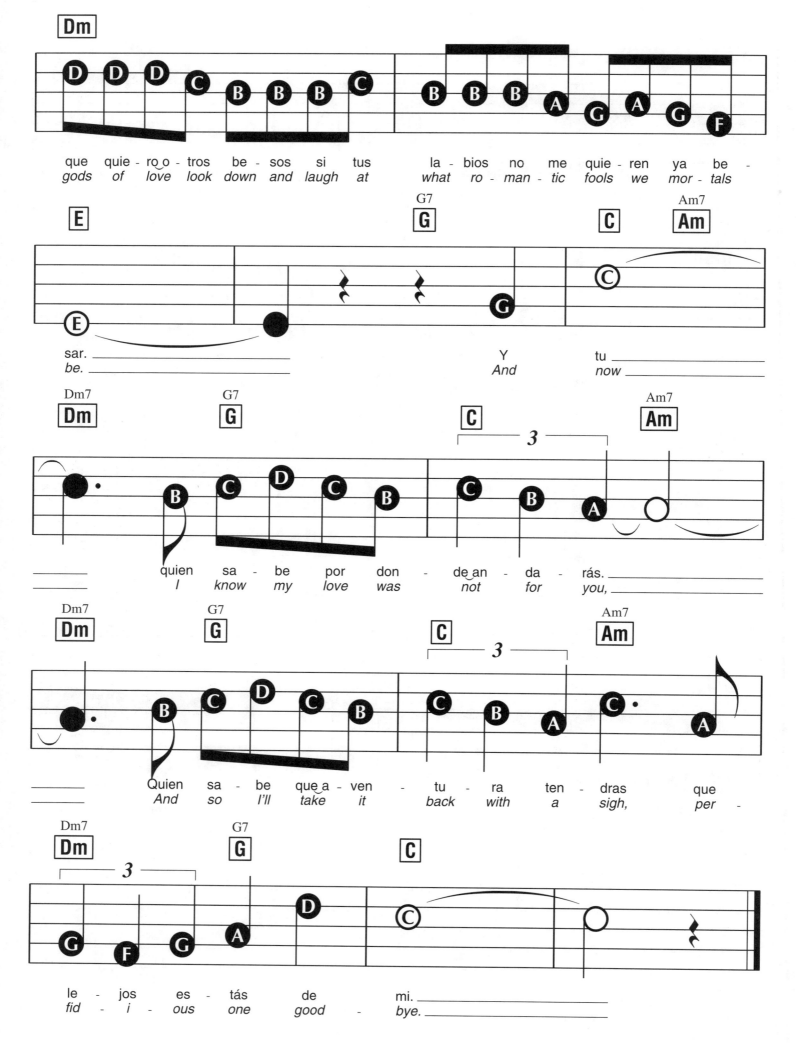

Quien Será
(Sway)

Registration 2
Rhythm: Rhumba or Latin

English Words by Norman Gimbel
Spanish Words and Music by Pablo Beltran Ruiz

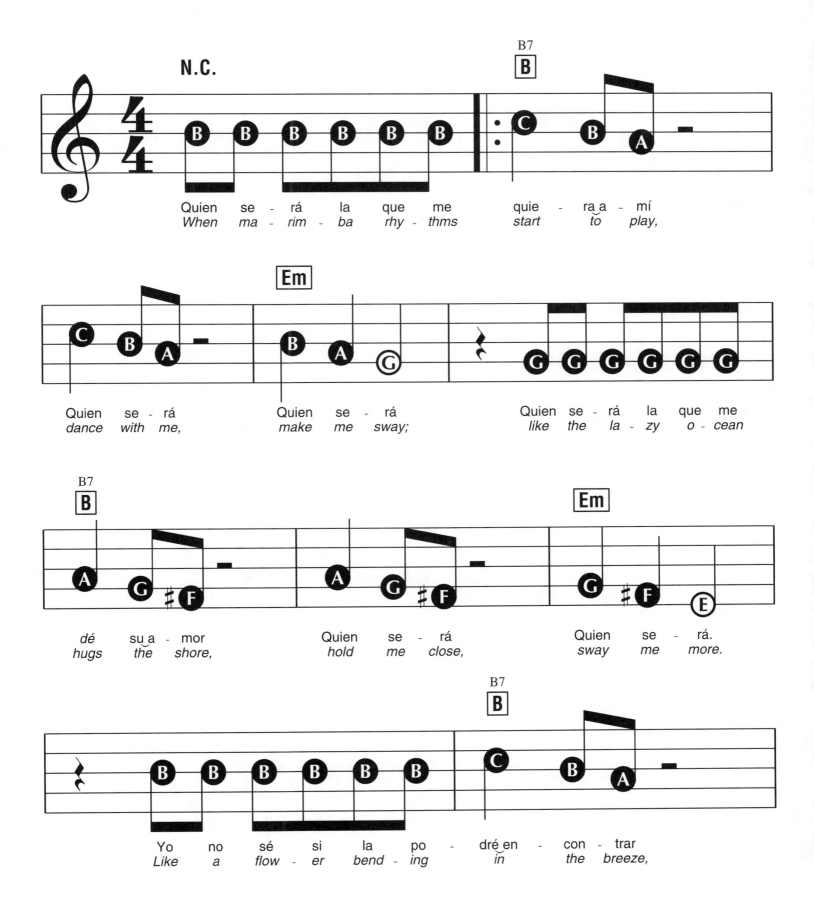

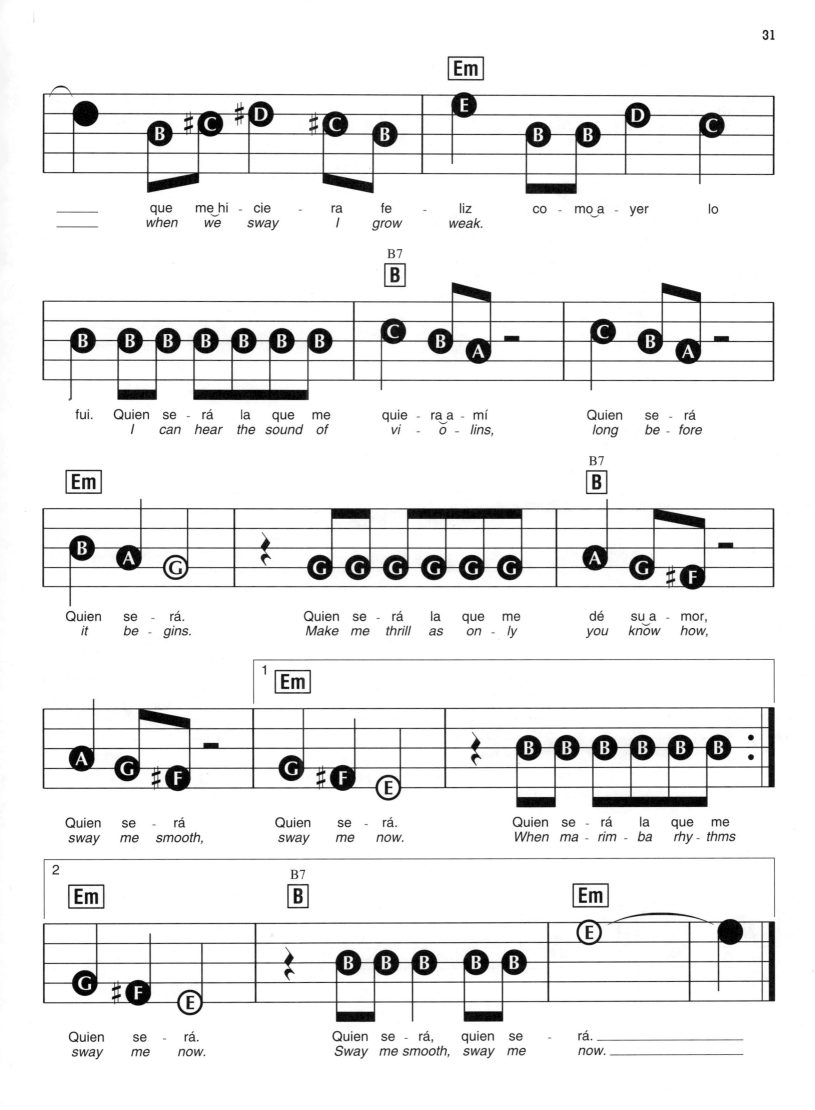

Sabor A Mí
(Be True to Me)

Registration 3
Rhythm: Rhumba or Latin

Original Words and Music by Alvaro Carrillo
English Words by Mel Mitchell

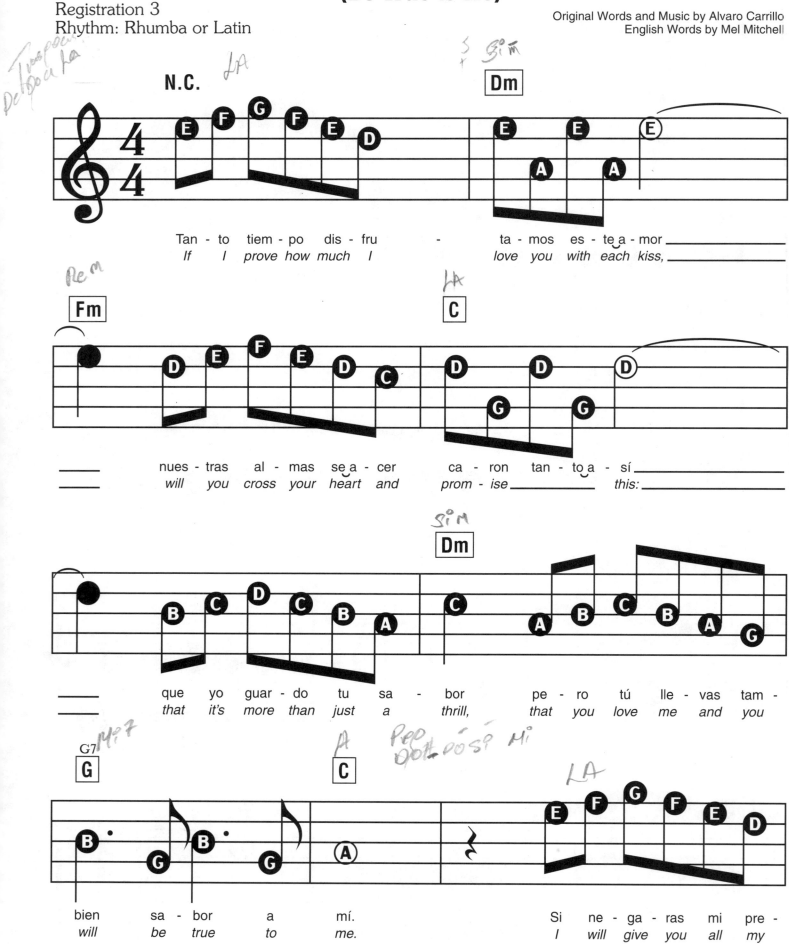

33

Siempre En Mi Corazón

(Always in My Heart)

Registration 4
Rhythm: Rhumba or Latin

Music and Spanish Words by Ernesto Lecuona
English Words by Kim Gannon

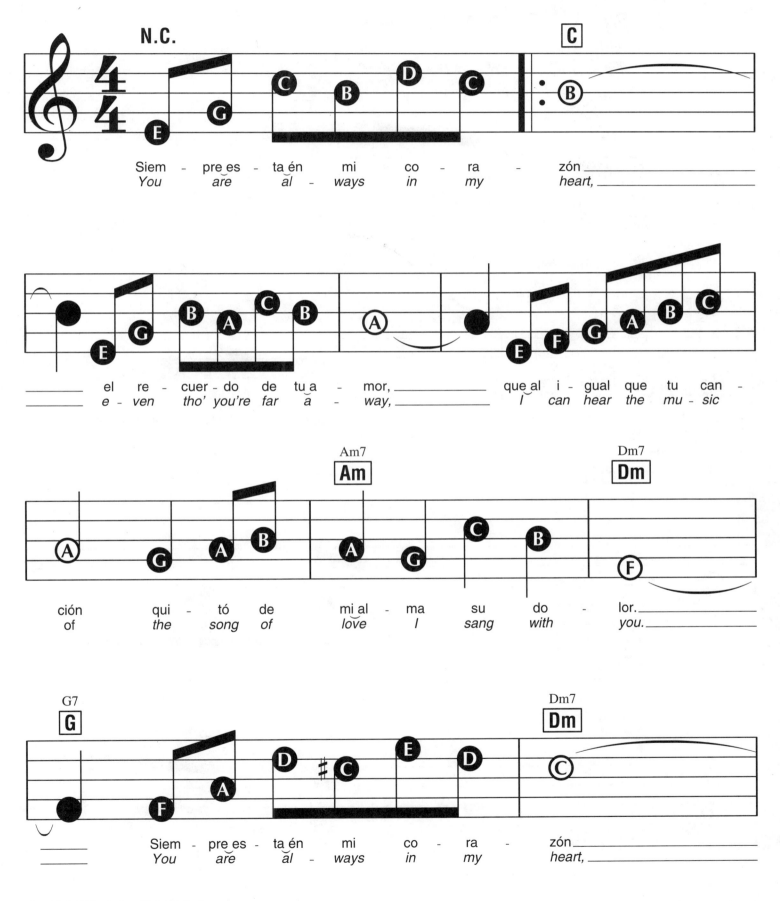

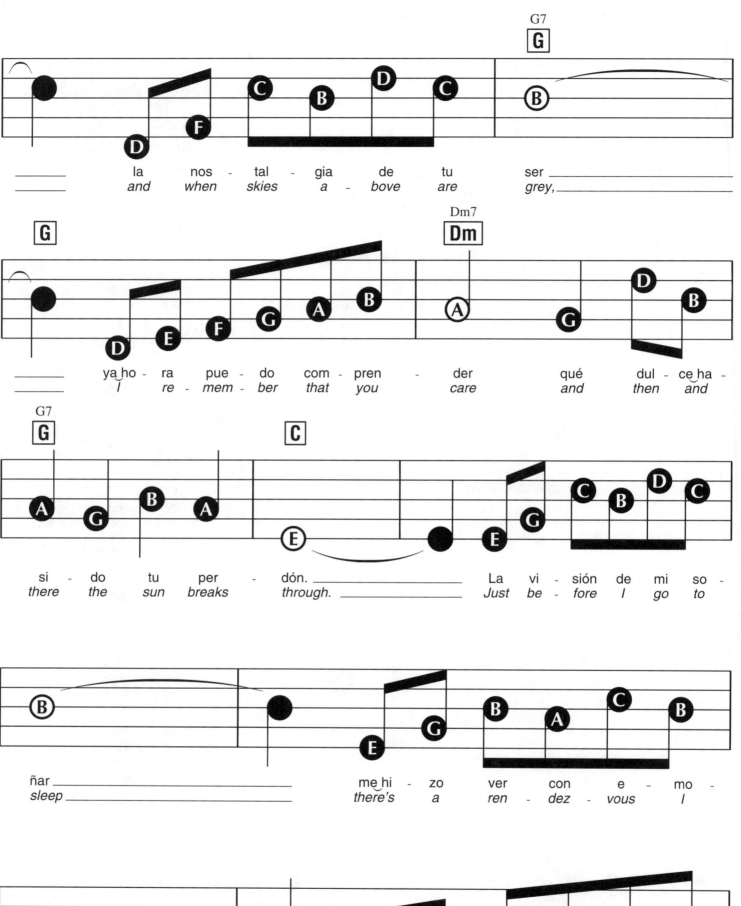

la   nos - tal - gia   de   tu   ser _____
and when skies   a - bove are   grey, _____

ya ho - ra pue - do com - pren - der   qué   dul - ce ha
I   re - mem - ber that you   care   and   then and

si - do tu   per - dón. _____   La   vi - sión de mi so -
there the tu per breaks through. _____   *Just be - fore   I   go to*

ñar _____   me hi - zo   ver   con   e - mo -
sleep _____   *there's   a   ren - dez - vous   I*

ción, _____   que   fue tu al - ma ins - pi - ra -
keep. _____   *And   the dream   I   al - ways*

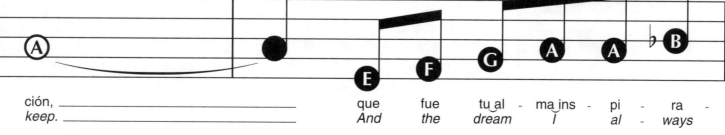

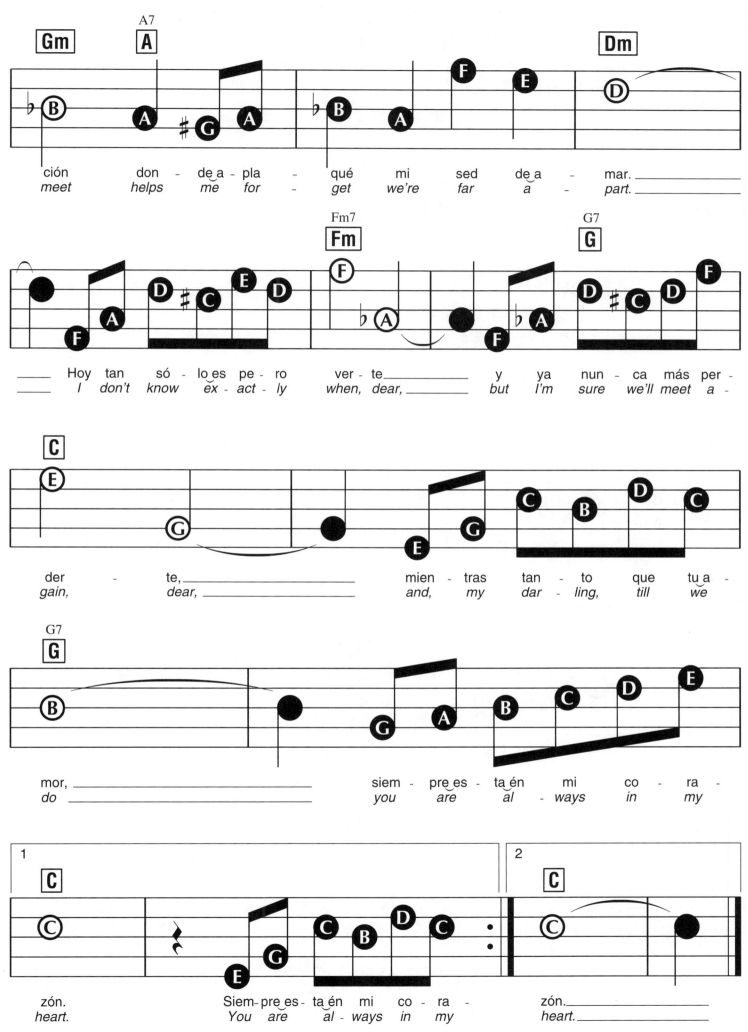

Solamente Una Vez
(Only Once in My Life)

Registration 5
Rhythm: Rhumba or Latin

Music and Spanish Words by Agustin Lara
English Words by Rick Carnes and Janis Carnes

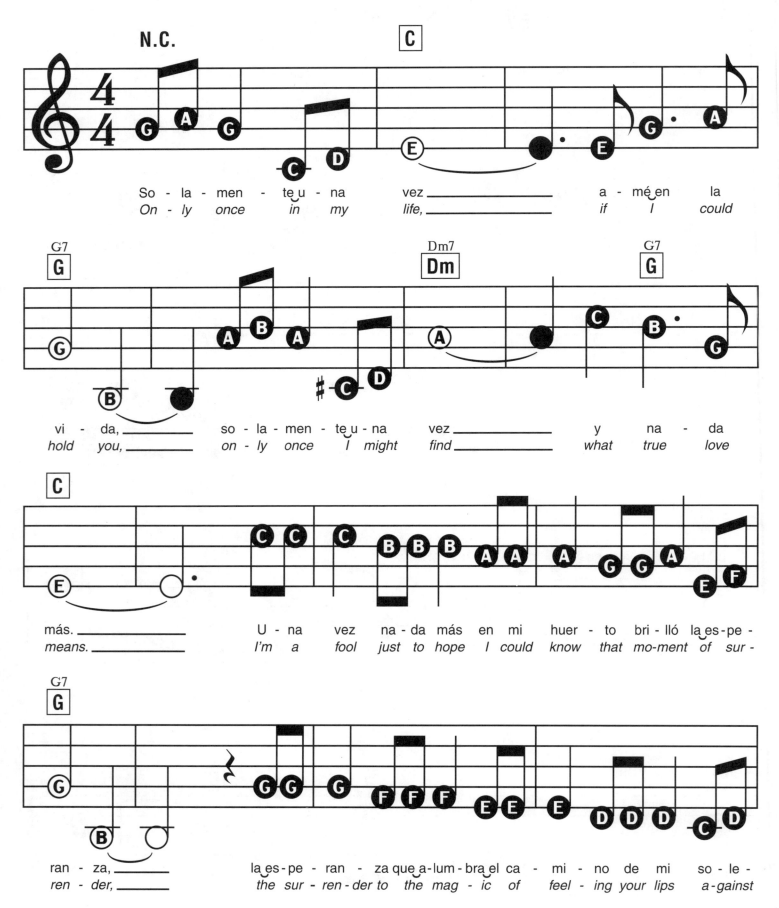

So - la - men - te_u - na vez _____ a - mé_en la
On - ly once in my life, _____ if I could

vi - da, _____ so - la - men - te_u - na vez _____ y na - da
hold you, _____ on - ly once I might find _____ what true love

más. _____ U - na vez na - da más en mi huer - to bri - lló la_es - pe -
means. _____ I'm a fool just to hope I could know that mo - ment of sur -

ran - za, _____ la_es - pe - ran - za que_a - lum - bra_el ca - mi - no de mi so - le -
ren - der, _____ the sur - ren - der to the mag - ic of feel - ing your lips a - gainst

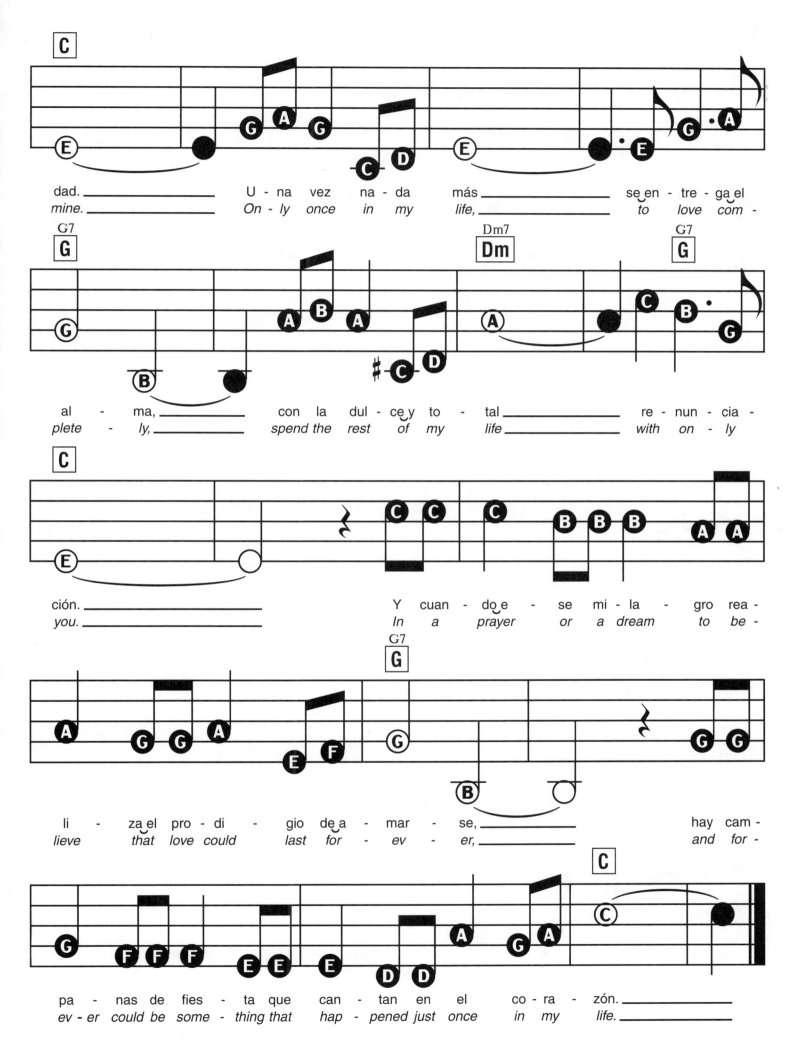

Somos Novios
(It's Impossible)

Registration 4
Rhythm: Rhumba or Latin

English Lyric by Sid Wayne
Spanish Words and Music by Armando Manzanero

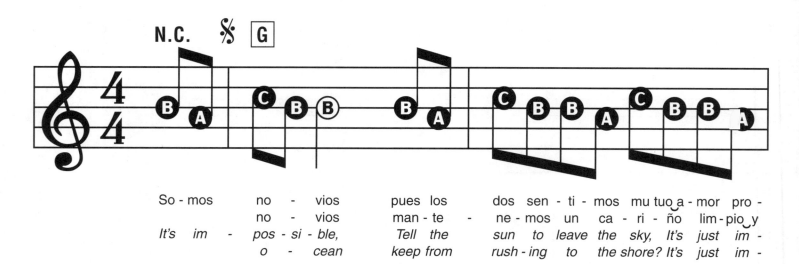

So - mos no - vios pues los dos sen - ti - mos mu tuo a - mor pro -
no - vios man - te - ne - mos un ca - ri - ño lim - pio y
It's im - pos - si - ble, Tell the sun to leave the sky, It's just im -
o - cean keep from rush - ing to the shore? It's just im -

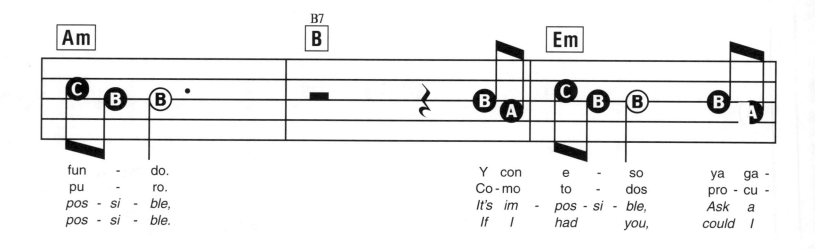

fun - do.
pu - ro.
pos - si - ble,
pos - si - ble.

Y con e - so ya ga -
Co - mo to - dos pro - cu -
It's im - pos - si - ble, Ask a
If I had you, could I

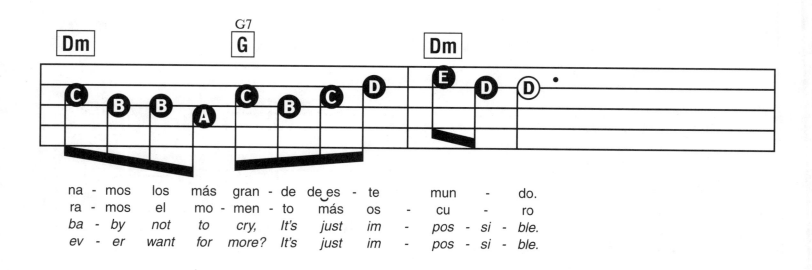

na - mos los más gran - de de es - te mun - do.
ra - mos el mo - men - to más os - cu - ro
ba - by not to cry, It's just im - pos - si - ble.
ev - er want for more? It's just im - pos - si - ble.

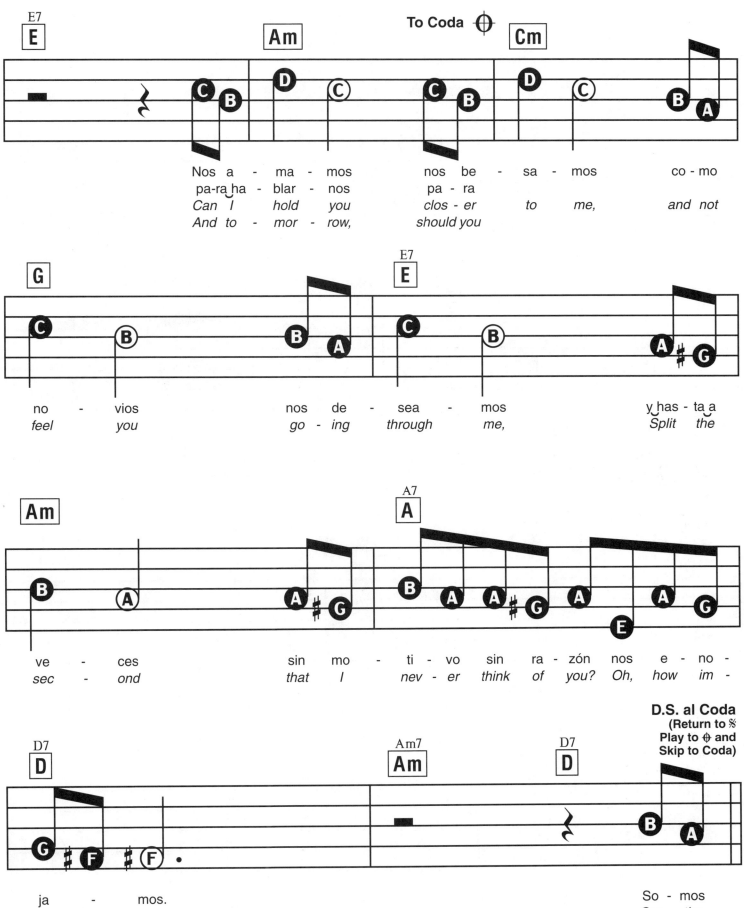

Todo Y Nada

Registration 6
Rhythm: Rhumba or Latin

Words and Music by
Vincente Garrido

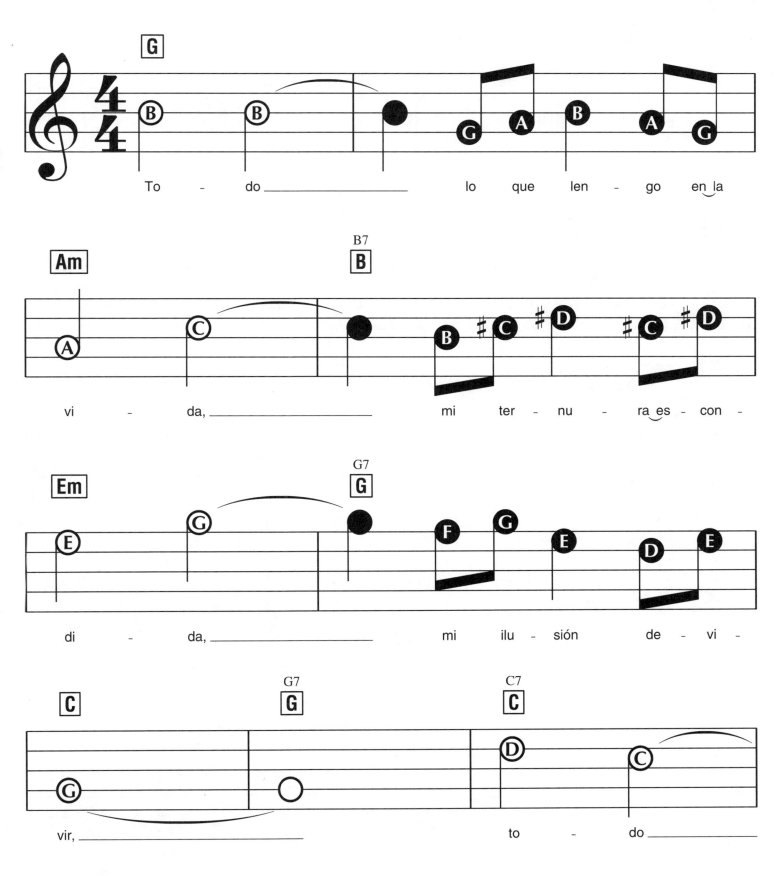

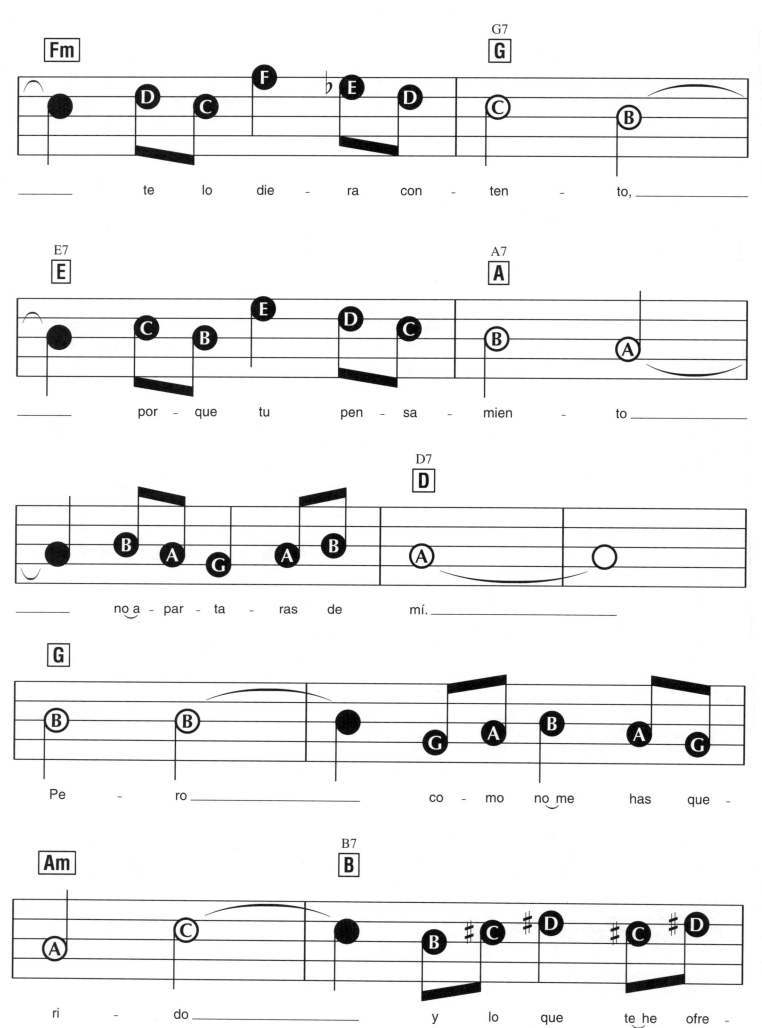

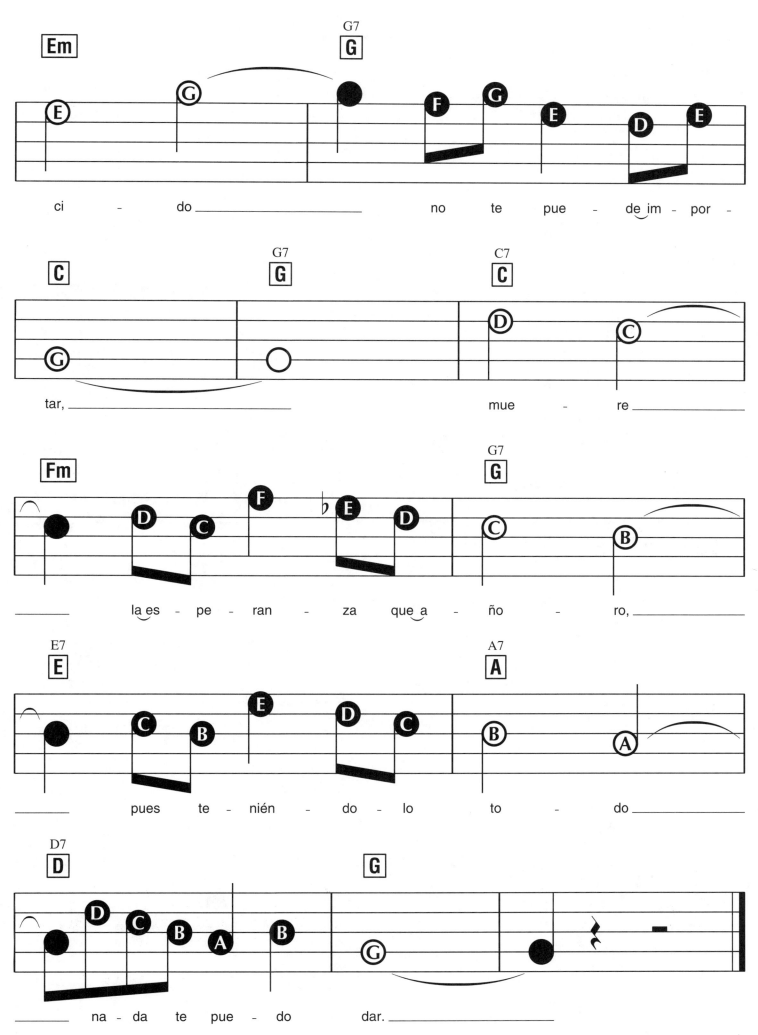

Tu Felicidad
(Made for Each Other)

Registration 4
Rhythm: Rhumba or Latin

Original Words and Music by Rene Touzet
English Words by Ervin Drake and Jimmy Shirl

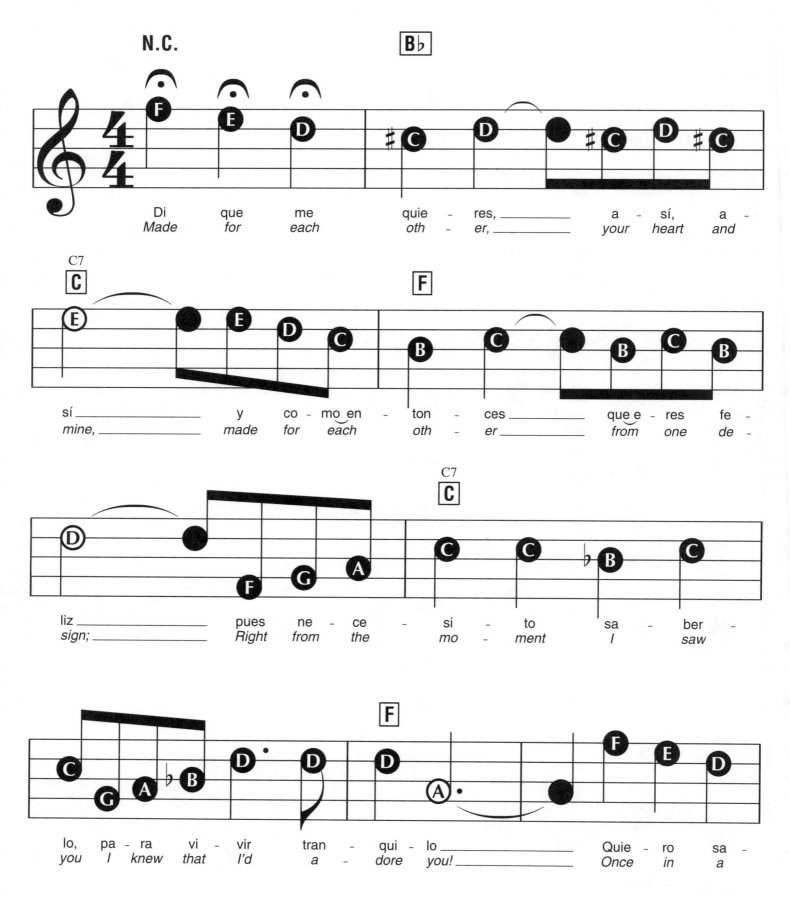

47

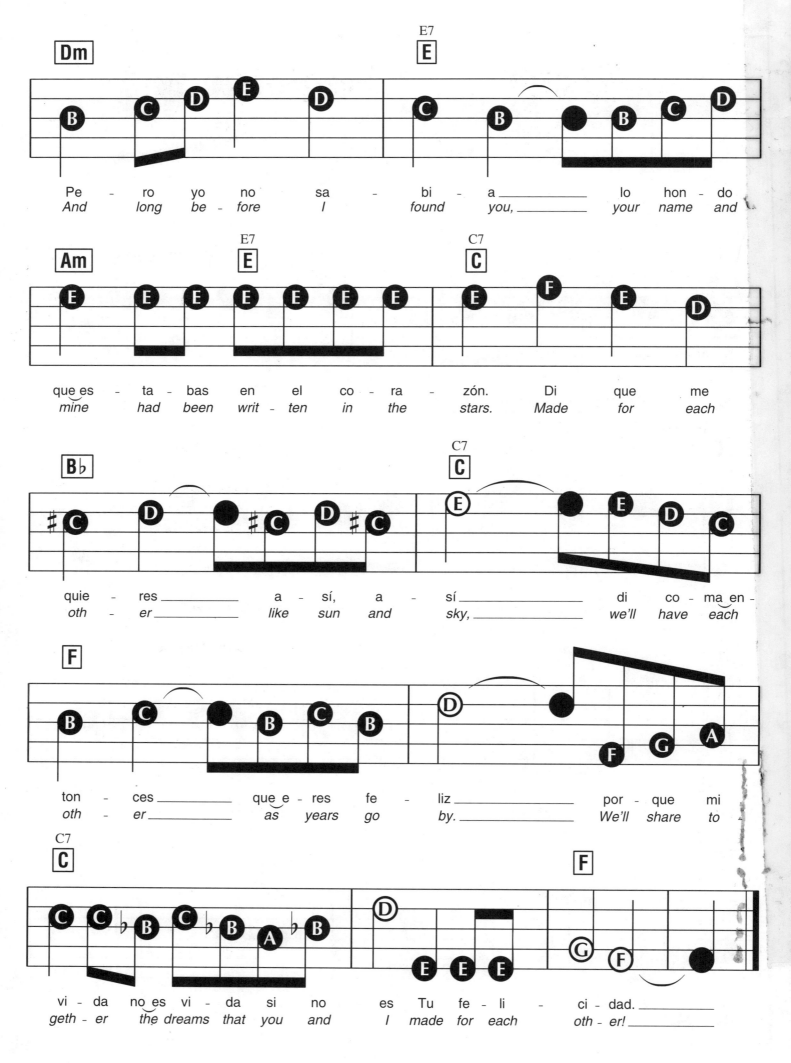